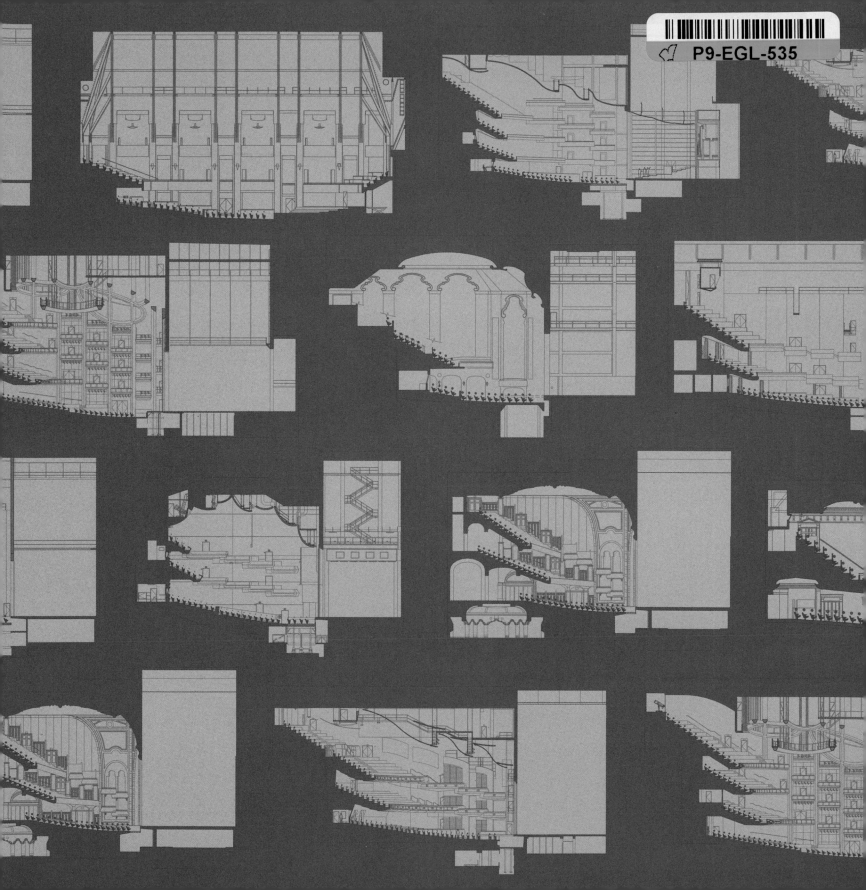

Theaters 2

Theaters 2

PARTNERSHIPS IN FACILITY USE,

OPERATIONS, AND MANAGEMENT

Holzman Moss Architecture

JaffeHolden

Theatre Projects Consultants

images
Publishing

Published in Australia in 2009 by
The Images Publishing Group Pty Ltd
ABN 89 059 734 431
6 Bastow Place, Mulgrave, Victoria 3170, Australia
Tel: +61 3 9561 5544 Fax: +61 3 9561 4860
books@imagespublishing.com
www.imagespublishing.com

Copyright © The Images Publishing Group Pty Ltd 2008
The Images Publishing Group Reference Number: 857

National Library of Australia Cataloguing-in-Publication entry:

Title:	Theaters 2 : partnerships in facility use, operations, and management / compilers Holzman Moss Architecture, JaffeHolden and Theatre Projects Consultants.
ISBN:	978 1 86470 3436 (hbk.)
Subjects:	Theater architecture. Centers for the performing arts. Theater management.
Other Authors/Contributors:	Holzman Moss Architecture. JaffeHolden. Theatre Projects Consultants.
Dewey Number:	725.822

Coordinating editor: Andrew Hall

Designed by The Graphic Image Studio Pty Ltd, Mulgrave, Australia
www.tgis.com.au

Pre-publishing services by Splitting Image Colour Studio Pty Ltd, Australia
Printed on 150 gsm Quatro Silk Matt by Everbest Printing Co. Ltd., in Hong Kong/China

IMAGES has included on its website a page for special notices in relation to this and our other publications.
Please visit www.imagespublishing.com.

Contents

Contributors

Debra Waters, LEED AP

Debra Waters, a Principal with Holzman Moss Architecture, has been responsible for the facility programming and planning of numerous performing arts centers in both civic and campus settings. She authored the Introduction to the companion publication, *Theaters*, 2000, as well as "Campus Cultural Facilities," a chapter of *Building Type Basics for College and University Facilities*, 2002.

Mark Holden, FASA

Mark Holden, FASA, is the Chairman and lead designer of acoustics at JaffeHolden. During the last three decades, he has forged successful working relationships with many of the world's leading architects and project designers to develop acoustical environments for major orchestral halls, theaters, and museums throughout the world. Mark applies his unique skills as an engineer, physicist, jazz musician, communicator, and collaborator to create superior acoustic environments. He has authored several papers for major trade publications and lectured at prestigious universities across the United States. He is a member of the National Council of Acoustical Consultants and a Fellow of the Acoustical Society of America.

Malcolm Holzman, FAIA

Malcolm Holzman, FAIA, is a founding Partner of Holzman Moss Architecture and a founder of Hardy Holzman Pfeiffer Associates. Throughout his 42-year career he has planned and designed some of the most celebrated performance facilities throughout the United States. He is an industry expert as recognized by the conferment of the 2006 United States Institute of Theatre Technology Distinguished Achievement Award in Architectural Design of Theatres. He has written extensively about the subject of theater design and architecture, including an essay in *Theaters*, 2000.

Benton Delinger, ASTC

Benton Delinger is a Principal of Theatre Projects Consultants and the Director of Project Management; with more than 10 years experience as a theater planner and project manager, he is well versed at working on projects with multiple partnerships. Before joining Theatre Projects, Benton spent many years working in regional theater as a stage manager, production manager, and a sound designer. He has twice served on the United States Institute of Theatre Technology Architectural Awards Jury and regularly speaks on panels at industry conferences including the Society for College and University Planners, International Society for the Performing Arts Foundation, and the United States Institute for Theatre Technology.

George Austin

George Austin is the President of the Overture Foundation, a private foundation created to provide support for cultural arts facilities in the Madison, Wisconsin area. The Foundation was the sponsor and developer of the Overture Center for the Arts in downtown Madison.

Richard Buckley

Richard Buckley is a renowned American conductor heralded by critics across the world for his passionate conducting style in both the orchestral and operatic genres. He served as Artistic Director of Austin Lyric Opera and continues his work in Austin as Principal Conductor.

Richard Dresser

Richard Dresser is a playwright whose work is widely produced in New York, various regional theaters, and in Europe. He recently completed a trilogy of plays about happiness in America. In addition to his work in the theater, he is active in film and television.

James Baudoin

James Baudoin is Project Director for the Performance Center of Asheville in North Carolina. He previously served as the Executive Director of the RiverCenter for the Performing Arts in Columbus, Georgia and as Executive Director for the Arts of Collin County, Texas.

Plácido Domingo

Plácido Domingo is an internationally celebrated singer and conductor, who also serves as General Director of the Washington National Opera and the Los Angeles Opera. Within the past few years he has been named one of the Kennedy Center Honorees; Commander of France's Legion of Honor; is a recipient of the Honorary Knighthood of the British Empire; has been awarded the highest decoration in the United States, the Medal of Freedom.

Jack Finlaw

Jack Finlaw is Director of the City and County of Denver's Division of Theatres and Arenas, which manages and operates such public assembly facilities as Boettcher Concert Hall, the Ellie Caulkins Opera House, the Buell Theatre, and Red Rocks Amphitheatre. Prior to joining the City, Finlaw served as the Chairman of the Board of Directors of Opera Colorado.

Doug Fitch

Doug Fitch has directed and designed opera for Santa Fe Opera, Los Angeles Opera, and Tanglewood and has created concert theater productions for the Royal Stockholm Philharmonic, the New York Philharmonic, and the Los Angeles Symphony, among others. As an artist-in-residence, he has worked with Bard College and Maryland University, developing new experimental performance projects with puppetry and live animation techniques.

Ed Herendeen

Ed Herendeen is Artistic Director and founder of the Contemporary American Theater Festival, one of America's most important producers of new work. He has also worked in a variety of regional theaters, and has served on the admissions committee at New Dramatists, NYC and as a panelist for the National Endowment for the Arts.

Anthony Sargent

Anthony Sargent is General Director of The Sage Gateshead. A Fellow of the Royal Society of Arts and an Honorary Fellow of the Birmingham Conservatoire of Music, his career includes arts roles with BBC Radio and TV, London's South Bank Centre, and the Birmingham City Council.

Rob Gibson

Rob Gibson is a producer, educator, and the Executive & Artistic Director of the Savannah Music Festival. He was the founding Director of Jazz at Lincoln Center, which became the world's preeminent presenter of jazz activities, and served on the faculty of The Juilliard School.

Susan Hilferty

Susan Hilferty is a costume designer, set designer, director, and Chair of the Department of Design for Stage and Film at NYU's Tisch School of The Arts, where she is involved in building what will become the new home of the Tisch Institute of the Performing Arts.

Howard Shalwitz

Howard Shalwitz is co-founder and Artistic Director of the Woolly Mammoth Theatre Company. Both an actor and director, Howard has also worked with many New York and regional companies including Playwrights Horizons, New York Theatre Workshop, Arena Stage, and Milwaukee Rep.

Bill and Sandra Gilliland

Bill and Sandra Gilliland are long-time residents and civic leaders of Amarillo, Texas who spent the better part of five years committed to bringing into existence the Globe-News Center for the Performing Arts. Both serve on the Board of the Gilliland Family Foundation.

Bruce LaRowe

Bruce LaRowe serves as the Executive Director of The Children's Theatre of Charlotte. This professional theater for youth is housed in ImaginOn: The Joe & Joan Martin Center and offers a comprehensive array of performances, education, in-school, and touring programs. LaRowe was formerly Associate Director of the Arts and Sciences Council of Charlotte-Mecklenburg.

Frank Turner

Frank Turner, FAICP, is Executive Director of the Development Business Center for the City of Plano, Texas and coordinates planning, engineering, capital projects, building inspections, and property standards programs, including revitalizing downtown to achieve a mixed-use transit oriented urban center.

Neal Gittelman

Neal Gittleman is the Music Director of the Dayton Philharmonic Orchestra. In previous positions with the Oregon Symphony, Syracuse Symphony, and Milwaukee Symphony, he observed and participated in two major hall renovations, which helped him play a leading role in the creation of Dayton's Schuster Center for the Performing Arts.

William Reeder

William Reeder is Dean of the College of Visual and Performing Arts at George Mason University and serves as CEO of Mason's two regional performing arts centers. Formerly, he was the founding President of the Sallie Mae Trust for Education, Vice President of the Washington Performing Arts Society, President of the St. Louis Conservatory of Music, and Executive Director of the Levine School of Music and the Newark Community School of the Arts.

Duncan Webb

Duncan Webb, President of Webb Management Services, Inc., has been a management consultant for the development and operation of performing arts facilities for 20 years. He has produced theater, taught at New York University's graduate program in arts administration, and is the author of *Running Theaters: Best Practices for Managers and Leaders*, published by Allworth Press in 2005.

Introduction

by Debra Waters

The cost and complexity of constructing, operating, and maintaining contemporary theater spaces almost necessitate partnering. Flexibility in performance spaces, sophisticated stagecraft, heightened audience expectations, and demand for large seating capacities all contribute to escalating costs and were not primary considerations for clients of past eras. It has become altogether uncommon for a presentation space to be erected to serve the single purpose of a specific user group. A performance space may serve a community fifty years or more if well considered before it reaches the end of its useful life, so maximizing its potential from the start is essential. This potential is both one of program and one of funding, and likely to inspire more partnering in the future. Such alliances usually involve an assembly of owners and operators; most host a variety of presentation types; and many bring together what might seem as disparate activities into a collaborative, experiential setting.

In 2000, I wrote the introduction to *Hardy Holzman Pfeiffer Associates: Theaters*, a publication that included the architectural work of more than thirty HHPA arts facilities, alongside essays by those intimately connected with the world of live performance, including actors, directors, scenic designers, producers, and critics. Contributors shared insights into what makes the theater-going experience memorable.

Theaters 2, by contrast, is not about the qualitative environment per se, but about the entities which bring it into being. While configuration, decoration, and technics continue to shape the theater-going experience, that experience is first defined by an interested client. To meet contemporary demands and aspirations, today's client is more likely a partnership of institutions, municipalities, agencies, or arts organizations, rather than an individual owner. So too, the vision for the performance hall is more often a space that caters to multiple user groups in many configurations and not a traditional room dedicated for theater, music, dance, or film alone.

The essays presented in this provide examples of some of the jointly used and funded performing arts facilities that Holzman Moss Architecture, JaffeHolden, and Theatre Projects Consultants have been involved with worldwide. Some of these unite academic and professional programs, or coalesce nonprofit arts organizations, while others bring together varied community arts and educational institutions, or county, city, and state client groups. They provide opportunities otherwise considered unfathomable, yet also pose considerable challenges which continually demand balanced resolution. Most importantly, they bring the promise of live performance in spaces that amaze and delight.

Partnerships on the client end set their sights on a broad vision in conjunction with specific needs. They are complex structures founded upon business plans, which carefully consider and document the agreement among parties, whether financial, managerial, or organizational. Partnerships among the planning and design team members, while also necessitating a working relationship based on mutual respect, are actually more fluid. Innovation and design excellence arises out of an open, exploratory process where expertise and experience are merely a starting point. There is a constant questioning of all that has come before, and a desire to reinterpret and advance the presentation environment for the benefit of performers and audiences alike. When successful, these theaters and associated public spaces fulfill the needs of varied users, from local businesses, to touring Broadway shows, school dance troupes, professional symphonies, college music majors, and community theater groups.

Partnering occurs on multiple levels. While it begins with the association of the client group, this group in turn assembles a team of consultants, which includes any number of specialties, such as architecture, theater technology, acoustics, cultural planning and management, engineering, and a host of other disciplines. Holzman Moss Architecture, JaffeHolden, and Theatre Projects Consultants have collaborated on many occasions in the planning and design of performing arts spaces. It seemed only natural therefore that we would partner in the publication of *Theaters 2*, and invite leading voices in theater partnerships to join us in this venture.

Top: Wachovia Playhouse, ImaginOn: The Joe & Joan Martin Center
Above: Texas A&M University-Corpus Christi

Malcolm Holzman

Holzman Moss Architecture

The arts influence the cultural ethos of an era and then years later reflect it to future generations. A persuasive account of this process is Tom Stoppard's recent drama, *Rock 'n' Roll*. It is a meditation on 25 years of Czech history, rebellion, and liberty at the end of the 20th century refracted through the prism of popular music as a 21st-century remembrance. Since the time of recorded public events where audiences gathered for the presentation of the spoken word, music, or dance these offerings have formed a basis of social tender. The exchange between presenter and audience is still one of pleasurable expectation. Today, the focus of these gatherings remains an individualized experience even though the types of performances, the places for gathering, and the sophistication of presentations are different.

Many aspects surrounding a performing arts event endure unchanged, from the heightened anticipation prior to attending a presentation to the occasional suspension of disbelief during a performance. Other aspects have been transformed in ways not anticipated; consider today's augmentation of natural acoustics with sound enhancement systems or the utilization of digitally controlled projected scenery. Theater architecture has evolved from outdoor presentations, to the use of indoor palatial rooms for the aristocracy, to black boxes that attempt to eliminate all references to the outside world.

Gathering in an auditorium has moved beyond the bounds of performances for theater, music, dance, film, and opera. New media, performance art, and mixed media events are occurring alongside traditional presentations. Contemporary spaces for events must be multipurpose to accommodate the widening range of offerings, the variety of presenters, and the shifting boundaries of performance itself. Partnerships between users of an auditorium are growing exponentially.

A particular representation characterizing this change is found in the design of multipurpose auditoriums even when the hall may be for a single use, such as music. Embracing a multitude of users from a soloist to a jazz band, accommodating natural and amplified sound equally well, is the common challenge in these facilities.

At Texas A&M University - Corpus Christi, a fledgling music program existed alongside a strong theater program. The local symphony performed in an undistinguished downtown performance space that did not adequately showcase guest artists. A generous donor and the state of Texas provided the funds for a new 1,500-seat performing arts center on the university campus.

Today the University music program is 82 percent of the hall's usage. Recitals and concerts related to academic programs constitute only one part of the facility's primary uses; it also produces an annual series of performances of internationally recognized artists and serves as the principal performance venue for the Corpus Christi Symphony Orchestra's annual concert season. Outside groups such as the United States Air Force Band of the West, the annual Buccaneer Classic Music Festival, local non-profit ballet and opera companies, numerous regional and state high school bands and choirs, and the Alpha Kappa Alpha Ebony Fashion Fair appear regularly on stage. This array of events brings a diversity of academic and community audiences to campus for a season that includes more than

200 presentations a year. By using adjustable acoustics and special lighting this single hall accommodates a variety of programs that could not have come together in an acoustically excellent Corpus Christi environment just three years ago.

A second type of partnership equally influences the design of auditoriums: collaborations among different civic groups or academic organizations. This evolution in both the shared use of space and the forces that partnerships generate alters, without apparent conflict, the physical characteristics desired in presentation halls. This directly affects building design and construction.

Two distinguished Charlotte, North Carolina civic organizations embarked on a partnership in 1997 to augment their already strong community programs. The Children's Theatre of Charlotte and the Public Library of Charlotte and Mecklenburg County joined forces to initiate a unique young people's program. Under one roof the spoken, written, and electronic word are programmatically interwoven. During its second year of operation, in 2006, these previously successful programs reached new heights by attracting 500,000 participants to special events, exhibits, and performances for young audiences and families.

At present, the design of auditoriums requires organizing community constituents first and then creating building projects. Partnerships take time to organize. The period of pre-design time dedicated to this germination period is usually referred to as the program development. It allows for discussion and debate about the potential uses of the facility and the relationships among users prior to starting architectural design.

Top left: 15,000-seat theater, Syracuse, Italy, 5th C. BC

Top right: *Metamorphosis*, 200-seat flexible theater, Del and Lou Ann Weber Fine Arts Building, University of Nebraska, Omaha

Above: Tuning concert, Texas A&M University-Corpus Christi

Joint users of a presentation space or an entire building need to understand the implications of the shared use. These range from defining operations of a larger facility than either partner might have previously required, determining the need for specific technologies that allow for new possibilities of presentation, and scheduling of events for participating user groups, to cite a few common topics. The reason organizations make these collaborative efforts is the transformative affect it can have on the participants and their communities.

Learning to share the wealth and divide the expenses, thus changing the scale of operations and management, is not a slow, steady progression; it requires a leap of the imagination and a lack of jealousy. An organization considering a partnership needs to first understand the limitations of acting individually and then find practical ways to judge the partnership to determine whether it can transform and enhance each member, while instituting long-term relationships. The process often begins by identifying essential goals that benefit the partners and the community they serve. Joint programs usually define new opportunities and often a new focus for activities. This global understanding is the essential key to a partnership from which other important detail topics flow. Evaluating existing spaces or deciding to construct new ones can only be determined after common goals are established. Once the framework is in place, concerns about potential sources of funding, form of administration, and business operations can be considered.

The impact of partnerships on their communities and the auditoriums designed for them can far exceed those that these same individual groups and organizations had in their previous

Above: Opening ceremonies, ImaginOn: The Joe & Joan Martin Center

years of operation. Individual groups linked by a common policy often accrue tangible benefits, from the symbolic importance of the partnership, to the depth and extent of the successes, the ability to easily stage events, and the magnitude of special events. No set formula exists for these shared undertakings. They are initiated and achieved by the sheer power and pioneering motivation of individuals and organizations that want to serve their communities in better ways. Architects too must rise to the challenge by addressing new kinds of client needs. They are called upon to provide new and expanded services to assist in reconciling budgets and program activities, building consensus among various groups, and fundraising—frequently before a design is prepared for a project.

Francis Marion University, a four-year, public South Carolina institution, formed a partnership with a local foundation, the city of Florence, and the state to locate its new performing arts center downtown to help spur the community's rejuvenation. A 900-seat multipurpose hall, a 100-seat black box theater, and other teaching, administrative, and support spaces are desired.

For the past half-century multiple types of presentations could only be accommodated in proscenium auditoriums by placing within the stage tower, at the proscenium opening, a series of elements that combined to form an acoustic shell for music. Once erected, this panelized shell appeared aesthetically different from that of the auditorium chamber. It takes considerable time to assemble, demount, and store the separate pieces of the shell; this is especially challenging if the stage is also used for rehearsal. Accomplishing this work can be expensive.

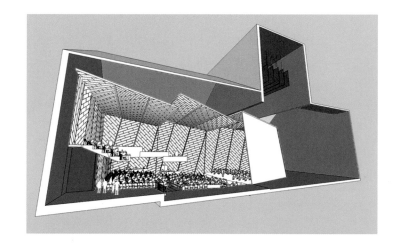

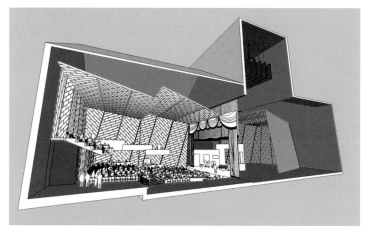

Top: Stage shell for concert performance, Center for the Performing Arts, Francis Marion University

Above: Stage shell stored for theater performance, Center for the Performing Arts, Francis Marion University

To provide for the variety of presentations requested by Francis Marion and the community, a significant departure from traditional music and multipurpose halls has been designed. The room incorporates an "actuated music shell" (patent pending). A single-piece shell, similar in appearance to the auditorium, moves from stage position to storage backstage in less than five minutes via a 20-ton crane. When tucked away in storage, the open stage and fly-loft can accommodate theatrical productions as large as Broadway touring shows. When the shell is in place for music, the seamless environment is scaled to accommodate a full audience house and through lighting, seating divisions, and materials even smaller audiences are made to feel comfortable.

To come to life architecture relies on human encounter and an individual's response to the shaping of space, the effect of light, the manipulation of scale, and the use of materials. Some contemporary theater presentations may seem at odds with architecture; I believe they both have the same objectives, making a unique experience. Theater architecture can be a set piece, a client may desire a "traditional" space with antecedents in the Renaissance or 19th century, but others may want spaces that are as plastic as the performance being presented. This is a challenge since architecture is most often immovable and unchanging. It does not need to be this way.

Theater design in the era of partnerships is shifting from providing an interior "wrapper" for the audience chamber, similar to the way a contemporary curtain wall provides the exterior wrapper for an office building, to becoming an

extension of the performance space. Sitting in a set piece—a large Neoclassical space (that is, the majority of Broadway theaters)—looking into a stage set, has evolved. In a black box theater or a small chamber music hall the audience and performer occupy one physical space with little or no architectural or scenic separation between them. The same type of walls, floor, and ceiling form a continuous enclosure surrounding a single activity, forging an intimacy not possible in other theater formats.

In large halls, relating the scale of the auditorium to that of the proscenium, which frames the stage performance, is not the only design approach open to theater architects. The most successful theater configurations visually and physically connect the presenter to the audience member and in doing so both promote intimacy and avoid the feeling of being in a neutral space. Just as actors and musicians on stage are made to appear "bigger than life" through the conventions of lighting, costumes, set design, and acoustics, audience members today are no longer thought of as an undifferentiated mass of individuals sitting in a darkened room looking into a stage with presenters.

Today the audience becomes bigger than life upon arrival at the front door of the theater. Multilevel lobbies provide the public with opportunities to observe and present themselves. Pre-performance, intermission, and post-performance time is choreographed. It allows for interaction among acquaintances as well as total strangers, a time for socializing, an opportunity for refreshments, and a chance for small, spontaneous presentations and encounters.

In the auditoriums we design, seating areas are frequently divided into sections. This serves to diminish the apparent scale of the room, accommodate audiences of varying size, and make the environment more comfortable. Every effort is made to populate the walls of the auditorium with audience members; people make better architectural decoration than inanimate materials. Boxes, side balconies, parterres, and slightly raised seating levels are a few of the devices used to provide an individualized audience experience. Lighting for the audience chamber can consist of more than one system. It is not unusual to have lighting systems designed for reading programs, but there are other special types of lighting used to enhance the audiences' appearance and add sparkle and drama to the space, heightening the sense that attending a performance is exceptional. Even in traditional auditorium formats, modifying the fixed proscenium opening with stage extensions reduces the visual barrier and brings the performer and audience in closer proximity.

A confluence of interrelated circumstances is the source of this evolution in partnerships, presentation, and theater design. Many large and small organizations and civic and academic presenters cannot afford to perform if the venue capacity is in some instances too modest or in others too big. Those who survive and better serve their communities are looking for changes and are often finding partnerships a satisfying solution. Many audiences around the world are being treated to intimate theater experiences at the same time as they are witnessing this unfolding of developments. An increasingly knowledgeable audience appreciates the difference.

Above: Opening ceremonies, Globe-News Center for the Performing Arts

Mark Holden

JaffeHolden

What is the relationship between a performance hall and sound? When you hear Beethoven played by a philharmonic orchestra in an acoustically grand hall, you are filled with a sense of awe. When that same performance occurs in an acoustically poor hall you hear a cacophony—it is disturbing. What is behind the scenes to ensure that your experience will be delightful, not dreadful? Acoustic challenges have become more extreme as theaters become multipurpose and are being built within larger mixed-use buildings/towers, in the center of cities, with many acoustical requirements. It has become necessary for the community constituents, the developers, different users, and design teams to make compromises and be ready for surprises. Over the course of 30 years of collaborating on the design of hundreds of buildings for the performing and creative arts, I can attest that the best buildings result from being ready financially, all players being involved early in the process, and establishing open and trusting partnerships. This is the key to a successful building that delivers architectural and acoustic results beyond the expectations of community constituents, the patrons, artists, and managers.

Acoustically, the widening programmatic needs can include anything from the speaking voice (such as theater), a philharmonic orchestra, a dance performance, an opera, a soloist, mixed-media productions, and your child's class performance, to unanticipated special events. Accommodating and adjusting the acoustics for these needs has become more frequent and necessary as theaters become a vessel for all types of audience–performer interaction.

The Long Center for the Performing Arts in Austin, Texas is located in a community that enthusiastically embraces both the traditional arts and cutting-edge performances. For example, a local theater troupe, the Rude Mechanicals, well known for "off the wall" theater using comedy and nudity, needed a home. The Austin Lyric Opera also needed a new home, apart from its limited facilities on the University of Texas campus, where it too could flourish. These and dozens of other Austin community users demanded technologically sophisticated spaces that would function exceptionally for natural sound and highly amplified events. The city of Austin had an underutilized civic auditorium overlooking Lady Bird Johnson Lake that it donated to a new, not-for-profit corporation chartered to build and operate the new arts center.

The partnership between the City, the Long Center Board, and numerous community and civic groups was difficult at times, and it took years and a false start to finally gel into the totally private-funded Long Center. In a city that is known by long time residents to be "terminally democratic," it is remarkable that the hall opened, on time and on budget, with Willie Nelson and the Austin Symphony performing on successive nights. Bikers in Harley Davidson leather jackets mingled with ball gowns and tuxes with amazing ease because the stakeholders made it a top priority to engage the community, the arts groups, and the Austin audiences in making the Long Center work brilliantly for every type of performance. The design of a successful building for the performing arts must be a holistic process and one where the acoustic design in the room is an integral part of the entire design. Acoustic treatments must contribute to the aesthetics, the functionality, and the feel of a space, rather than be an independent function that is layered on top of the design.

It is the acoustician's responsibility to be wholly involved in all aspects of the structure, exterior, interior, and finishes because acoustic requirements impact all materials and building systems.

This intensive involvement commences in the earliest phases of a project. The acoustician builds a "sound" relationship with the potential new users, the stakeholders, the architect, the theater consultants—the team needs to work harmoniously and efficiently. The acoustician collaborates with the theater consultant and architect to define the dimensions and proportions of every area where sound is critical. To fight off inflation, the team makes quick decisions rooted in goals and compromises set by the different constituents.

The idea for the new Zankel Hall to be located under the venerable Carnegie Hall in New York City came about though the collaborative vision of Isaac Stern and others on the Carnegie Hall Board. A third venue was needed to present artists in a more contemporary and intimate setting, where emphasis would be on ultimate flexibility of performance orientation and audience interaction. The result was a unique elliptical plan that defined the artists and audience in a rounded enclosure, fostering intimacy and contact between performers and audience. JaffeHolden supported this idea, but the concave warped walls would form acoustic anomalies, such as hot spots and dead zones in the audience. Rather than rejecting the concept as unworkable, we collaborated with the Carnegie staff and the team on the design, suggesting a more rectangular shape be incorporated within the ellipse, while retaining much of the bent walls at the corners of the room.

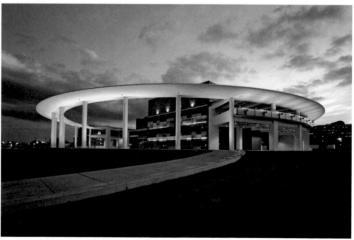

Top: Michael and Susan Dell Hall, Long Center for the Performing Arts
Above: Joe R. and Teresa Long Center for the Performing Arts

Top: Judy and Arthur Zankel Hall, Carnegie Hall
Above: Alice Tully Hall and the Juillard School, Lincoln Center

By leaning the inner rectangular walls at 7 degrees and cladding them in solid wood, the acoustic reflections on the inner walls were optimized for brightness and clarity of sound, reinforcing the visual intimacy and connection with the audience.

The acoustician's role has evolved to include more services that meet the needs of the ever-expanding partnerships. Fifty years ago, performing arts halls involved the collaboration of a dozen or so individuals. Today, it is a constituency of hundreds! The architects, acousticians, and theater consultants work carefully, often for five or more years, to discover the best route for each pipe and ventilation duct. As technology advances, the acoustician delivers the additional needed services in a clear and understandable manner that can be put to use immediately. This is of tremendous value to the project's success.

The artistic characteristics of acoustical design are embodied in the skill of applying the known criteria in proper proportion and measuring throughout the course of the design process and sometimes in discordance with the desires of other team members. When this creative tension occurs, the resourceful acoustician sorts out which acoustic goals are really important from what would be nice to have, but are not really essential. Then, the suitable and compelling point must be made with the team that this one aspect is worth the cost, the design team's effort, and the secondary effects on the building.

For the renovation of Alice Tully Hall at Lincoln Center in New York City, the team—one of the largest and most complex this author has ever worked with—collaborated on the creation of a unique and compelling new design for the interior of the revered hall. Lincoln Center is actually not one organization, but is composed of many boards and constituent group boards, and the Juilliard School, all with individual relationships to the Center. Alice Tully Hall, while located within the Juilliard School Building, is actually a separate entity.

While the structural "bones" of the hall (the balcony, floor, and ceiling) would need to remain, the interior skin was re-imagined by the architects to be a glowing vessel that surrounded the performers and the audience. Central to the design was the way the skin (the walls) would glow in a warm blush of color.

Acoustically this was extremely challenging. Walls need to be solid, substantially supported, and braced to create the good acoustic reflections and strong reverberation preferred by groups such as the Chamber Music Society of Lincoln Center and the Juilliard Orchestra. Materials that glow tend to be thin and unsubstantial, such as glass or plastic, which would take in sound in uneven and negative ways reducing the acoustic performance. Also, the New York subway tracks are only yards away from the building. The new interior skin would need to be mounted to prevent vibrations from the metal wheels on the tracks telegraphing into the renovated hall.

A truly collaborative design process emerged with the architects, lighting designers, acousticians, structural engineers, and manufacturers during the design phase. Scheme after scheme was put forth and mocked up with different materials, structural support systems, and lighting sources—then considered and refined by team members to achieve a workable and cost-effective solution that met all needs. All the schemes needed to

Above: Starr Theater, Alice Tully Hall, Lincoln Center

be reviewed by all the stakeholders and user groups, as well as the multiple boards and the Juilliard School. The solution was ingenious. To achieve the warmth and richness of a wood interior (wood is highly regarded by musicians and audiences for its acoustic response) and to get the wood to "glow," a thin veneer of wood was imbedded in a thick, heavy, and stiff clear resin and lit with colored LEDs from the rear.

The resin was tested in an acoustical lab to assess if it would perform the same function as plaster or solid wood in a more familiar concert hall design. Even the mock-up required a high level of collaboration and teamwork. The walls would undulate and warp, blending into the glowing portion, as if the hall was carved from a single block of wood 90 feet long and 80 feet wide. Additionally, the wall needed to limit subway vibration, be fire resistant, ventilated so the lighting does not overheat, accessible to change the light instruments, code compliant, structurally sound, able to be built within the time allotted and, of course, it needed to be on budget. Naturally the donors, users, and Boards wanted to see, touch, and suggest improvements to the mock-up. The end result is today one of New York's most successful new theater spaces.

Today, lobbies are much more than a space between the hall and the outdoors; they are performance spaces in their own right, hosting dinners, concerts, weddings, and receptions. Acoustic treatment can appear to be at odds with the hard glass, stone, and plaster favored in public lobbies. However, there is now flexibility in material selection; felt, acoustic plaster, and perforated metal can be used to good effect.

It was the desire of the Columbus State University's Schwob School of Music to move to downtown Columbus, Georgia. The facilities at the main campus were inadequate. They needed more teaching suites for professors, practice rooms, rehearsal halls, and most importantly, performance spaces for student and faculty recitals and concerts.

Civic, university, and government leaders saw an opportunity to partner on a new facility, the RiverCenter for the Performing Arts, which would meet multiple needs and become an important economic driver for the revitalization of the city center. The facility would be the new home for the university's music department, local symphony, and touring performances, and it would redevelop an unused downtown city property perfectly located between the convention center and the restaurant/retail corridor.

An extraordinary community-based fundraising campaign raised more than US$100 million to supplement public funds for construction and to provide ongoing endowment to ensure financial viability of the center. Input gathered during programming meetings from all potential users and stakeholders for new and flexible spaces was balanced with budget realities and the result was a compromise—one all could live with. Included in the RiverCenter structure is the 2,000-seat Bill Heard Hall, which excels as both the home to the Columbus Symphony and the university choral concerts, as well as hosting convention center sessions and touring Broadway productions. The 450-seat Legacy Hall is a recital space for use by visiting artists and the University. Its tunable ceiling can adjust sound to optimize acoustics for choral concerts of 100 singers, 12-piece jazz ensembles, and organ recitals. Legacy Hall and the facility's 150-seat, black-box Studio Theater provides rehearsal and performance space for the Columbus State University's Schwob School of Music. The School also uses the RiverCenter's classrooms, studios, rehearsal rooms, and practice rooms.

RiverCenter fulfills its mission of partnering with local performing organizations by serving as the home of the Youth Orchestra of Greater Columbus, the professional chorus Cantus Columbus, and the Columbus Ballet. It addresses its outreach mission through its ArtsReach program, offering area youth of all socioeconomic levels unprecedented opportunities to experience and participate in the arts. Operating as a non-profit organization, it also supplies theatrical, volunteer, security, and maintenance services for its home organizations. While providing quality entertainment and promoting the artistic enrichment of the Columbus area, RiverCenter has become much more than a great performing arts center; it is a key player in the preservation of the social, economic, and civic vitality of the region.

A new order of collaboration is happening. Buildings are built by people for people. A successful building is one that becomes more valuable and useable for the community as time goes on.

Above: Bill Heard Theater, RiverCenter for the Performing Arts

Benton Delinger

Theatre Projects Consultants

We are in the midst of a large and sustained era of building visual and performing arts centers, with new facilities arising all over the USA and around the world. In the future, we believe others will consider our present time as a significant period for the arts, similar to the vaudeville and movie palace eras of the last century. These buildings are being realized by both large and small communities as part of redevelopment/regeneration measures or as a significant investment in the arts.

This growth is not limited to civic arts buildings. Colleges and universities everywhere are rediscovering the importance of the arts in providing quality education for the next generation of leaders in our society. As a result, they too are embarking upon significant cultural buildings that welcome the local community and prospective and current students to campus.

The interesting part of what we are witnessing is the variety of different partnerships being developed. This new generation of arts centers is a very expensive proposition because they need to support such a wide range of performances, from natural acoustic events and amplified concerts to circus-type shows. These buildings require sophisticated mechanical systems to protect artwork and complex theatrical and acoustical equipment, none of which are simple to design or construct. More so, many different skills are called upon to successfully navigate the pitfalls of creating these systems. Partnerships are necessary to promote, fundraise, and support these future artistic centers.

All arts buildings begin with a vision and a partnership. The vision of what the arts mean to the community, and a partnership between artists, civic leaders, administrators, the design team,

and ultimately all of the trades people who will build the facility. Each individual person or group will provide their money, insights, and skills to support the vision. From these partnerships, cities are regenerated and enlightened with the arts.

We have seen any number of partnerships formed, including:
City, county partnerships
County, state partnerships
Multi-city, county, private partnerships
Artists, city and private funding partnerships
Foundations, city, state, artistic, and educational partnerships

People arrived at these partnerships to make buildings that enhance and reflect their communities. They are centers of activity; provide spaces for artists to create, perform, or display their work; and become beacons of pride for towns, cities, colleges, and universities.

We frequently see these partnerships in urban renewal projects. Such projects often require a long-term vision, in some cases 15 to 20 years, of what the future can be and rock solid faith in that vision. Around the world we have seen the addition of an arts facility successfully jump-start regeneration efforts, from The Sage Gateshead in Gateshead, England, which revitalized a rundown part of the city; the San Jose Repertory Theatre (Holt Hinshaw Architects) in San Jose, California, USA, which created a central home for the arts on a path that leads from the center of education (San Jose State University) to the center of technology (World Headquarters of Adobe Systems); and the Esplanade in Singapore, which developed a new part of the city; to the Shaw Center for the Arts (Schwartz/Silver Architects with

Eskew Dumez Ripple) in Baton Rouge, Louisiana, USA, which launched a classic urban regeneration project. Each of these facilities helped transform its community into a center of entertainment, serves as a catalyst for future growth, and demonstrates civic pride.

As projects have more stakeholders involved, the need for a wider range of theatrical equipment solutions is required. Each group expects the spaces to fully support their type of programming. The job becomes more challenging as we try to provide contemporary multi-use space that works extremely well for music, dance, opera, or amplified events. The need to easily adapt spaces to different performance types has resulted in the expanded capabilities and complexity of theatrical systems. At the Kimmel Center, Inc. in Philadelphia, USA, a large turntable was required to transform the smaller performance space from recital hall to theatrical road house at the push of a button. For the renovation of a church at Northeastern University, it was the delicate coordination of adjustable acoustic banners within the historic building structure that challenged our creativity. For some buildings, the design team needs to provide several spaces that are each tailored to a specific type of use, from a small drama space or a concert hall. For other buildings, they must provide several different types of rehearsal spaces. Each solution is reached by keeping the needs of the different constituencies in mind and requires careful thought and attention to budget.

The Shaw Center for the Arts in Baton Rouge, Louisiana is a recent example of the power of arts buildings to change the social fabric of a downtown core and become a town center.

Top: Shaw Center for the Arts
Above: Douglas L. Manship, Sr. Theater for the Visual and Performing Arts, Shaw Center for the Arts

Top: Esplanade – Theatres on the Bay
Above: The Sage Gateshead
Right: San Jose Repertory Theatre

This modern facility came out of a study that identified and confirmed that a new arts center would be a vital addition to downtown. At the time of the study, downtown Baton Rouge had lost most of its retail and restaurants. All of it had fled, like most cities, to the suburbs. The new center is located across the street from the old state house, an icon of the past now standing opposite a vision to the future. Civic leaders combined the programs of a revitalized downtown into one facility: a new museum for Louisiana State University, a new community theater, a studio theater, a rehearsal hall, and new opportunities for retail, restaurants, and outdoor activities. Each space was created with the needs of very different groups in mind, and each equipped to support small presentations and local touring musical acts.

To successfully build it required close collaboration among the State of Louisiana, the City of Baton Rouge, Louisiana State University, and the Baton Rouge Area Foundation. This many organizations can often prove unwieldy, but with commitment to the singular goal of creating an arts center as a beacon for the whole community, these groups not only were responsible for selling and supporting the vision to the community but also providing the funding for the capital costs. These same groups continue to be a part of the ongoing funding and operations of the facility, demonstrating that this wonderful addition to their community is an outcome of their steady involvement.

When the Shaw Center opened in the spring of 2005, the partnership had achieved their goal. It included not only the theaters and an art museum, but also a gift shop on the ground floor and a signature rooftop restaurant overlooking the Mississippi. During construction, work began on other area projects as a direct response to their vision of the future of downtown. They had hoped the Shaw Center would be a magnet for revitalization but had no idea that it would also become the center of activity and information for displaced Louisianans after hurricanes devastated New Orleans and other southern parts of the state in the fall of 2005. Since that time, Baton Rouge has grown by more than 50,000 residents and is now the largest city in Louisiana. The facility has been able to support the community because of its location and its iconic status.

In our office, a lot of time is spent discussing the importance of the theatrical experience and how we want buildings to function. How does a person get from their home to their theater seat in the best possible frame of mind to see the performance or the visual art being presented? We spend hours agonizing over how to assist in the creation of lobbies that are hubs of animated social activity, the intimacy of auditoriums that support both the artists and the audience, the back of house spaces that are great places to work, and the technical equipment that makes everything sparkle and dance. Our goal is to help to produce a building that is remembered by the people who visit and perform, and that enhances, reflects, and transforms its community and the artists within.

We recently returned to the Shaw Center and saw firsthand the development that had occurred in the last two-and-a-half years. The transformation of this part of downtown has been dramatic. In 2004 it was very difficult to find a place to eat after 3pm in the afternoon. In 2008, the Center has a coffee shop and two restaurants open with a third on the way. Across the street a Hilton Hotel revived a historic hotel. Activity during the week, from morning to night, is a wonderful sight to see. It has brought together students, citizens, theatergoers, and art lovers from all around the region to this part of Baton Rouge. Theater people mix with students who mix with government employees on the roof of the building over drinks. The theater program that was almost put on hold after the hurricanes has come roaring back from not one subscriber to the beginning of a healthy base with a very bright future.

The Shaw Center's success confirms that a tremendous vision of community regeneration enacted with a strong partnership of city officials and civic leaders can create a new destination for old and new citizens alike.

Rob Gibson

Throughout history, music has been performed and enjoyed in a variety of settings dependent upon its function. Whether sacred or secular in nature, music has informed, transformed, entertained, amused, or enlightened people at churches, theaters, ceremonies, picnics, parades, concert halls, dance halls, pubs, clubs, bars, bordellos, and, in more recent times, arenas and stadiums. No matter how modern our world becomes, the experience of live music remains irreplaceable. And while our interaction with artistry connects us with what it means to be human, it is more precisely the setting in which we encounter music that facilitates its ultimate spiritual or dramatic effect.

The opportunity to create a space for the musical arts is a rare occurrence that first demands a valid artistic program or conception, followed by a thorough cost analysis, requisite funding, and much planning. In the 21st century, nearly any concert hall or theater constructed for musical purposes must have multiple functions and be designed for different musical genres. For example, a great room for symphonic music should also accommodate recitals, chamber music, jazz, lectures, and possibly even dance, film, or theatrical productions, without ever compromising its primary function. Not only is this important in order to afford and maintain such a facility, but also to ensure that the space is used by multiple organizations, which ultimately means more life for the arts.

Devising, designing, and building such spaces involves hiring a group of professionals who specialize in architecture, theater

Left: Starr Theater, Alice Tully Hall, Lincoln Center

planning, acoustics, or construction. This team must be properly managed and inspired in their work together to ensure that the project achieves its potential as an extraordinary place that stimulates successful relationships between artists and audiences, while also effectively serving producers, administrators, technicians, and staff.

Assembling the design team requires a clear understanding and delineation of each person's role in the project. Because architects, theater planners, and acousticians often possess similar skill sets and knowledge but have different aesthetic sensibilities, determining who will "shape" the space is a major decision. Affecting the design are such factors as intimacy, flexibility, access, expenses, and income (ticket sales). Whether the space is a 300-seat theater or an outdoor pavilion accommodating 12,000 people, it should have great sound and sightlines, function well for any event, and offer pleasurable and memorable experiences.

Paramount to making these spaces successful is the motivation and leadership of the architectural team during the most important phases of the project: planning, schematic design development, design development, and construction documents. The creation of a performing arts venue is so specialized that it often takes a very personal commitment from each consultant, who consistently pushes for what he/she believes to be the best solution, often leaving the client to manage competing views and make the final and most informed decision.

The key to any project's success is effective communication both within and outside the organization. Holding meetings with clear agendas, showing respect for everyone's time, and building consensus from within not only keeps key players involved, but also saves money in the long haul. The desired result is a space that feels intimate, looks unique, and sounds wonderful, thus providing a personal connection between the audience and the artist.

While serving as Executive Producer and Director of Jazz at Lincoln Center (JALC) in New York City (1991–2000) our organization was selected by Mayor Giuliani to be the cultural centerpiece of the largest multiuse development built in Manhattan for many years—the Time Warner Center at Columbus Circle. The complexity of the development meant

that six architectural groups worked concurrently on separate projects in a mixed-use skyscraper that included retail shops, a hotel, condominiums, and corporate offices. JALC had its own myriad experts and consultants charged with creating unprecedented rooms for jazz music, all set above one of the busiest subway stations and traffic locations in the city. Throughout the early planning and design phases, the major challenge was to establish the presence of our organization inside the massive development, which would ultimately serve as a catalyst for the revitalization of Columbus Circle and the surrounding neighborhood at the southwest corner of Central Park.

Left: Grand Foyer, Alice Tully Hall, Lincoln Center
Above: Conical sound diffusers, Starr Theater, Alice Tully Hall, Lincoln Center

Our vision was to construct a state-of-the-art performance complex (Frederick P. Rose Hall), conceived for the function and feeling of jazz, engineered for warmth and clarity of sound, and wired for the latest technology. The most significant expansion of Lincoln Center—the world's largest and leading performing arts center—in more than a decade, it included separate musical spaces on the 6th floor: a 1,200-seat theater (Rose Theater), a 500-seat space with a 90-foot window overlooking Central Park (The Allen Room), a 140-seat club (Dizzy's Club Coca-Cola) that would present jazz every day of the year, and rehearsal rooms/recording studios all acoustically isolated from one another.

Throughout the project, JALC Artistic Director, Wynton Marsalis, maintained that our goal was to make each space work first and foremost for "the sound of jazz." Because jazz primarily uses non-amplified instruments with distinctly different volume levels based around a rhythm section (piano, bass, drums), it has unique sound characteristics. Thus, we sought to create rooms possessing great clarity of sound that would unite musicians and concertgoers no matter whether the musical performances were acoustic or lightly amplified. In order to further the feeling of jazz, a fundamental goal of the design was intimacy, whereby we could bring everyone as close to the stage as possible, surrounded by as many people as could comfortably fit into the space.

Rigorous studies, meticulous calculations, and several years of intense discussions preceded the design of some of the finest sounding rooms. The two large spaces have variable properties that utilize ambitious design elements such as a retractable concert shell ceiling, mechanical tiers, and a sophisticated acoustical curtain and banner system to help tailor sound qualities for individual performances. In the Rose Theater, 11 movable on-stage seating towers were created to allow for a variety of seating configurations that create both a "theater-in-the-round" for concerts or, when stored against the back wall, make way for a traditional proscenium stage accommodating opera, theater, film, and dance. Ultimately, the team was able to create the world's premier jazz performance hall, but one that accommodates a variety of performing arts.

Left: Grand Foyer, Alice Tully Hall, Lincoln Center
Above: Starr Theater, Alice Tully Hall, Lincoln Center

Participating in the creation of this facility has served me well as director of the Savannah Music Festival (SMF) since 2002, especially in my involvement with the transformation and development of Trustees Garden. This historic property in Savannah was begun as an experimental farm in 1734 during the founding of Georgia and comprises 10 acres with several older buildings. The site's first facility to be reconstructed in 2008 is the Charles H. Morris Center, an 1871 building that now serves as a flexible 300-seat space for a variety of concerts, dances, films, lectures, and parties. It is yet another SMF performance setting that also includes theaters, auditoriums, rotundas, places of worship, club-styled spaces, and outdoor venues in Savannah. Our association in such projects has provided us with a more comprehensive understanding of how best to utilize and transform spaces, allowing us to continue connecting artists and audiences in a combination of exciting ways.

Top: Dee and Charles Wyly Theatre, Dallas Center for the Performing Arts

Above: Margaret McDermott Performance Hall, Margot and Bill Winspear Opera House, Dallas Center for the Performing Arts

Right: Margot and Bill Winspear Opera House, Dallas Center for the Performing Arts

Top left: Margot and Bill Winspear Opera House, Dallas Center for the Performing Arts
Left: Rehearsal Hall, Dee and Charles Wyly Theatre, Dallas Center for the Performing Arts
Above: Potter Rose Performance Hall, Dee and Charles Wyly Theatre, Dallas Center for the Performing Arts

William Reeder

Northern Virginia is a land of paradox. The historic home of George Washington and George Mason, the region boasts a rich cultural tradition and in the last decades of the 20th century began discovering rapid economic growth and increasing international diversity. Located in the shadow of the nation's capital, the region is shaped by a series of edges—between towns and counties, countryside and cityscape. Rural and southern roots blend with international cosmopolitan activity. Some parts of the region are awash with cultural amenities. Others are awash with artists, but seriously deficient in professional arts facilities.

By the late 1990s, one such fast-growing region—Prince William County—had matured to the point that it needed a high-quality performing arts center to serve its own communities, as well as to attract visitors to the area. In response, Prince William County, the city of Manassas, and George Mason University (a public university), advised and assisted by individuals from the private sector, formed a partnership to create the region's first performing arts center—a project designed to educate, entertain, and enrich the lives of its residents—and to give resonance to their artistic creativity on many levels.

The process led to an agreement among the three partners (Prince William County, the City of Manassas, and George Mason University) to finance the design, construction, and furnishing of a Community Performing Arts Center. The original agreement called for a US$56 million project. Design and

Left: Merchant Hall, Hylton Performing Arts Center, George Mason University

construction was estimated at US$36 million. Based on projected utilization, partner financial participation was allocated at 60 percent for Prince William County, 30 percent for the University, and 10 percent for Manassas. The university contributed the land, construction management and fundraising management. The university will "own" the center, and be responsible for its management and operations. A board comprising proportional representation between the partners and the community will oversee policy formation and the fiscal health of the center.

The partnership agreement also stipulated that a US$15 million permanent endowment be raised from the private sector. When fully in place, the endowment, along with annual fundraising, would allow the center to close the annual operating gap between anticipated earned income and operating expenses. After the partnership agreement was signed, inflation increased the design and construction budget from US$36 million to $44 million. The additional US$8 million has been raised from the private sector, as well as a grant from the state government.

Successful partnerships begin with an answer to the question: "What could we do together that we could not do alone?" Looking back over the past six years, since a group of Prince William County community leaders and university officials answered this question, five "lessons from the field" have emerged that seem relevant to the success of the partnership.

First, leadership matters. In our case, the specific individuals who stepped into leadership roles were genuine trusted agents within their own organizations, as well as broadly viewed throughout the community as trustworthy and reliable. Without doubt the single most important factor in establishing the partnership was the personal trust the leaders of each jurisdiction—the county, the city, and the university—held for the other, and the ability each leader had to work both internally and externally for the partnership. This trust had developed over many years with numerous shared projects and activities. Beyond trust, the leaders of the partnership held a deeply shared vision for the future of the region and for the role that a cultural facility would play in economic, social, and cultural advancement. Perhaps most importantly, the leaders

needed to represent both the aspirational goals for their constituent communities and to make large financial and legally binding commitments on behalf of the partnership.

Second, the project must meet the independent strategic goals of each partner, and form a new interdependent whole. This requires that the partners commingle people from each organization not only for the strategic planning of the partnership but for the strategic plans of each partner independent from the other. In our project, members of the university community served on citizen planning boards for both the county and the city in establishing multi-year budget priorities, which ultimately included support for the performing arts center. In turn, city and government officials became actively involved with the university's planning processes on a newly constituted arts board. The planning efforts lasted more than three years, resulting in a fully integrated and informed partnership with a strong sense of shared values and purposes where the arts center was concerned.

Left: Gregory Family Theater, Hylton Performing Arts Center, George Mason University
Above: Hylton Performing Arts Center, George Mason University

Top: Hylton Performing Arts Center, George Mason University
Above: Didlake Grand Foyer, Hylton Performing Arts Center, George Mason University

Third, we needed to make sure that we built the right building and that the performing arts center would respond to the strategic, social, artistic, economic, and cultural needs of each partner's constituent community. Here, the architectural team becomes an indispensable member of the partnership coalition. The skill of the architects in hearing, interpreting, and feeding back the needs and wants of the community through the design ultimately determines whether the partnership will succeed.

With the help of our architects, Malcolm Holzman and Doug Moss, and with the assistance of consultant Duncan Webb, the partners realized that three spaces were called for—an intimate 1,100-seat main hall, a 300-seat flexible theater, and a large lobby capable of addressing the social, business, and ceremonial needs of the community. The architectural team determined that we would want them to design and construct a space for use by school children, amateur artists, regional professional artists, international touring stars, and corporate presenters. We needed a space that would allow everyone from a 5-year-old beginner to a seasoned professional to both look and sound great. We needed corporate and civic meeting spaces. And, reflecting the artistic and cultural attributes of the region, we needed spaces that would work for everything from bluegrass to Beethoven, from the Virginia Cloggers to the Mark Morris Dance Group, from theatrical productions to solo recitals.

Most importantly, Holzman Moss Architecture recommended that we pull the back wall of the main auditorium close to the stage, wrapping around it with a series of opera house style boxes. What was once viewed as an elite style of architecture has now been recast in a series of "family boxes" where parents and children can attend in comfort with "wriggle room" for the youngest members of the crowd. While the auditorium is cozy, the stage and orchestra pit are full sized, capable of supporting the largest ballet company, a combined orchestra and chorus, a school musical, or touring opera. Through the design features of the building, the strategic requirements for each partner have been successfully embraced—but throughout the process the partners needed constant feedback, reminding, and architectural inspiration.

Fourth, the governance and management of the facility need to accommodate the unique requirements of each partner. These include legal documents, ownership agreements, bonding and financing arrangements, construction management, operations, programming, and board tasks and responsibilities. Each dimension must be fully described and accountability firmly fixed. Great care must be afforded in the flow of information. Transparency of each and every dimension is paramount.

Finally, new models of governance and of management need to be explored. Blending three governmental agencies, a research university, and the community into a new enterprise represents true innovation and exciting answers to the original question: "What could we do together that we cannot do alone?" At George Mason, we have created the Arts@Mason Partnership, which expresses a relationship between the university, the community at large, and artists (both professional and amateur). In support of the partnership we have evolved a cluster of "Friends of" groups around the disciplines of music, art, dance, theater, film, and arts management. We have drawn the leaders of these friends groups, along with people from the political and regional jurisdictions we serve, into the Arts@Mason Board.

The great management teacher, William Oncken, Jr., once observed that there are four things partners are seeking to experience. First is a chance to contribute something that the partner values in his or her own eyes. Second is for that contribution to be recognized as having made an important difference. Third, that the environment of the partnership is relatively stable and predictable. And finally, "when I tell folks that I am a member of the partnership team, I receive their admiring approval."

Looking ahead, the arts appear to be heading into a new golden age in Northern Virginia—and possibly across the nation. In his book, *The Rise of the Creative Class*, economics guru Richard Florida cites the strength and position of the arts sector as a leading indicator of a city's health and economic growth potential. The arts already possess intrinsic value; they inform and inspire us. Beyond that, it is now clear that the arts are part of the economic fuel for the nation, and

provide the "quality-of-place" that Florida asserts is necessary for cities and regions to compete for the creative workers that businesses now need.

But there is paradox in this new golden age. In the past, when we thought of growth in the arts, we thought of growing audiences and donors. Today, people are not only showing up at the box office, they are coming onto the stage as active participants. There is a new diversity model emerging as the new arts participants are of all ages, all levels of skill, and are seeking both the familiar and the new, a rich genre mix representing a global ethnicity.

As people move from the audience into active participation, we are seeing the birth of a whole new approach to sustaining arts experiences, with a set of large questions emerging about physical spaces, operational and programmatic priorities, funding, artistic and social intentionality, and governance models. If we are to respond to the 21st-century tidal wave of arts participants—and if we are to fully embrace what active arts participation means for society—increasingly partnerships are the way to go.

Doudna Fine Arts Center, Eastern Illinois University
Charleston, Illinois, USA

Left: Recital Hall, Doudna Fine Arts Center, Eastern Illinois University

Above: Dvorak Concert Hall, Doudna Fine Arts Center, Eastern Illinois University

Top left: Doudna Fine Arts Center, Eastern Illinois University

Top right: Proscenium Theater, Doudna Fine Arts Center, Eastern Illinois University

Above: Black Box Performance Space, Doudna Fine Arts Center, Eastern Illinois University

Right: Lobby, Doudna Fine Arts Center, Eastern Illinois University

Bill and Sandra Gilliland   47

Amarillo, Texas is a city of 200,000 people located in the far northern tip of the state. Our small city, which has a symphony orchestra, ballet, and opera company, has always been remarkably supportive of the performing arts. "Amarillo needs a world-class, acoustically correct performing arts center," was the exact statement Carol Emeny made to my wife and others ten years ago. Carol, a long time supporter of the arts, backed the statement with a US$7 million commitment (thus becoming our anchor donor), if I would agree to chair the effort. To her, my wife and I were a logical choice to work on this project as we possessed many years of experience in economic and cultural involvement in the community.

Our small group realized that a project of this magnitude would require the concerted efforts of many people. "The project would never have happened without the Gillilands," commented Mary Emeny, daughter of the philanthropist and an active board member. From a small group of interested and active individuals a groundswell of support developed. A foundation to advocate an arts center quickly developed and a Board of Directors for the non-profit organization began to lead the efforts. Quickly partnerships and relationships were formed, composed of key leaders from the arts and business communities. Within three months after Emeny announced her gift, about US$12 million had been raised. The final cost of the facility when it opened in 2006 was nearly three times that amount but still primarily paid for by private donations.

Left: Globe-News Center for the Performing Arts

"If we build the center and deed it to the city, will you operate it?" was the question posed to the city. The answer was a resounding yes. The city of Amarillo agreed to operate the facility after construction and fund any operational shortfalls from an existing tax stream. Our local newspaper, the *Amarillo Globe-News*, provided US$3 million for the naming opportunity. "Do business with people who buy their ink by the barrel," certainly worked well here. All of our performing arts groups, including the symphony, opera, and ballet companies provided specific recommendations and, more importantly, established "ownership" in the project. The city, which already operated the 2,000-seat Civic Center, became an active participant in the development of this complementary 1,300-seat hall, since it would operate both and have the same management, custodial staff, and stagehands.

Much of the money was privately raised from donors who were ardent supporters of the various arts groups. Because nothing in our region of Texas of this magnitude existed in which they could perform, a committee representing the various entities was formed. For the first time in our community, these groups worked together to make this structure become a reality, and their input was vital. Local non-profit organizations were assured that this project would be funded by large contributions and would not compete with their efforts. The partnership expanded to include the vital team of architects, engineers, construction managers, city oversight, and our organization who worked in close harmony.

Above: Multi-purpose education space, Globe-News Center for the Performing Arts

Right: Lobby, Globe-News Center for Performing Arts

Following pages: Concert Hall, Globe-News Center for the Performing Arts

Our goal, that the center exist for everyone, not just an elite few, was actively promoted by the local media. They regularly explained and told the story of our ambition. What was at first thought to be a "symphony hall" has in fact turned out to be a center for every kind of performances from western music, educational performances, high school music concerts, children's theater, poetry readings, musical groups of all kinds, and many more in addition to the symphony, ballet, and opera. Moreover, the Globe-News Center for the Performing Arts is serving as a catalyst for the revitalization of downtown Amarillo. For the first time in many years interest in a new hotel and other commercial developments near the center has come forward.

From the beginning of the fundraising process to build the Globe-News Center for the Performing Arts, the board, staff, and donors realized there was an opportunity through cultural programming to have a major impact on childhood learning. During construction more than US$1.3 million was given to the future education program. WOWW (Window on a Wider World), dedicated to enriching the education of Texas Panhandle students through arts, science, and cultural experiences, has been incredible. For many of the children's programs we are able to provide distance learning opportunities to our rural schools; we have also held physics classes on site. These are just two of the many

ways in which the Center serves to benefit elementary school students in the region.

We invite you to come visit our remote city and witness first hand our "world-class, acoustically correct" performing arts center. It is marvelous indeed!

Left: Globe-News Center for the Performing Arts
Top: Entrance, Globe-News Center for the Performing Arts
Above: Dressing room, Globe-News Center for the Performing Arts

Left: Lyric Theatre, Esplanade – Theatres on the Bay
Above: Esplanade – Theatres on the Bay

Above and bottom right: Lyric Theatre, Esplanade – Theatres on the Bay

Top right: Recital Studio, Esplanade – Theatres on the Bay

Top far right: Foyer, Esplanade – Theatres on the Bay

Left: Concert Hall, Esplanade – Theatres on the Bay
Above: Foyer, Esplanade – Theatres on the Bay

Bruce LaRowe

61

Imagine a new facility partnership with an architect, theater consultants, and acousticians. Add in a second architect and two clients: a public library (a department of local government) and a private 501c(3) children's theater. Does this sound like a prescription for bureaucratic gridlock and failure? A naïve Pollyanna dream? Or a "one-of-a-kind facility" in the country?

ImaginOn: The Joe & Joan Martin Center is the realization of these collaborating partners. Begun in 1997 as a dream to provide additional space for youth activities for the Children's Theatre of Charlotte and the Public Library of Charlotte & Mecklenburg County, North Carolina, ImaginOn has evolved into not only a shared facility for both organizations, but also a programmatic endeavor that is truly unique. With a mission of "bringing stories to life"—written stories of the library, spoken stories of the theater and electronic stories with cutting edge technology, ImaginOn engages visitors of all ages in a variety of programs and activities. Since opening in 2005, ImaginOn annually serves 500,000 young people, aged from birth to 18, and their families. It has garnered many accolades from children, adults, theaters, and libraries from across the country and, increasingly, from international visitors.

This uncommon collaboration is a resounding success, but that success is a result of years of advance planning and hard work and an ongoing commitment. Are there challenges as well as benefits to partnering? The answer is an emphatic "yes."

Far left: Lobby, ImaginOn: The Joe & Joan Martin Center
Top left: Wachovia Playhouse, ImaginOn: The Joe & Joan Martin Center
Left: Studio-i, ImaginOn: The Joe & Joan Martin Center
Following pages: ImaginOn: The Joe & Joan Martin Center

The structure of this partnership is as unique as the partnership itself. A Lease and Operating agreement details the legal relationship regarding the theatre, library, and ImaginOn. There is not a separate legal entity called ImaginOn. Rather, the public library and children's theatre are equal partners in the programming and operations of the facility. The public library owns the building and the children's theatre is a "tenant" by strict definition. Whereas the theatre pays US$1 in rent per year, the theatre and library split 50/50 the costs of operating and staffing the facility and conducting shared programs. These shared costs include utilities, maintenance as well as custodial, security, and programming staff. All programming and operating decisions for ImaginOn are jointly managed and supervised by the library manager at ImaginOn and the executive director of the children's theatre. In addition to this daily operating structure there is an oversight Management Committee that meets on a quarterly basis and reviews ImaginOn policies, budgets, and programs. The Committee comprises an equal number of library and theatre trustees and staff.

The formation and role of our building committee actually predated the creation of the Lease and Operating agreement, but follows the same philosophy and was the model for the Lease. All decisions regarding the design and building of ImaginOn were shared between the library and theatre. The initial building committee consisted of the library director and theatre executive director as well as additional staff from both agencies. The architect selection committee had six members, including both directors, two additional staff members, and a trustee from both the library and theatre. Ultimately, the library had hiring and veto authority, yet all decisions were able to be made by consensus and the architect selection and building design were jointly made in all instances.

Throughout the process the library was the owner and contracted with architects and construction parties. It is important to note that the theatre and library shared in design decisions as well as difficult "value engineering" decisions. The fact that selection, design, and budgetary decisions were jointly made is a testament to the commitment to the partnership on the part of both parties. It is a commitment shared by both governing boards and senior staff leadership.

What do we gain by partnering? The mission is paramount to both agencies and by staying focused on this mission we find that the benefits are impressive. The overarching guiding philosophy has been that the whole is greater than the sum of the parts. The program opportunities and potential for completely new offerings are apparent. A local author wrote both the book that was published by the public library and the play that was staged by the children's theatre. A page-to-stage exhibit was created and the author made numerous school visits demonstrating the literacy/writing/theater connection. The theatre produced a play on teenage social issues and the Teen Loft of the library brought in a nationally acclaimed teen author to speak. Both groups co-hosted talkbacks for teens after each performance of the production. By bringing two independent organizations into one space we maximize the strengths of both. We share resources, have synergy in vision and programs, and are better equipped to serve youth in innovative ways.

We have created a facility together that could not have been accomplished individually and we have capitalized on the strengths each partner brings to the table. The construction bond funding could only have happened through library participation; the theatre's role was coordinating the advocacy efforts for its passage. The theatre led the fundraising aspects of an endowment campaign that benefited both organizations. The library coordinated and led the efforts regarding facility construction because of their experience in building multiple branches; the theatre had no track record in this area.

What are the challenges or risks involved in partnering? There is mutual ongoing concern for agency identity and independent decision-making authority. The partners come from different cultures (government versus private non-profit) and the budget size is vastly different. Governing authority and internal processes reflect these cultures. Similarly, philosophies regarding free access versus fee for services had to be considered and worked out for the benefit of both partners and the constituencies we serve.

Right: Wachovia Playhouse, ImaginOn: The Joe & Joan Martin Center

Our experience has told us that the benefits far outweigh the challenges. What lessons have we learned through this process? We have learned that patience is not only a virtue—it is essential. More time is required to make decisions and more people are required to be at the table. Each individual agency decision must be looked at through the lens of the other agency and its impact on the partner. We must test all assumptions and check our personal agendas at the door without compromising our agency's integrity and mission. Compromise is not a dirty word—it is the creation of a win–win environment. One must be committed to the partnership and see the project through both the good and the difficult times, just like a successful marriage.

Finally, true partners must be willing to be vulnerable—to be open to change to allow ourselves and our agencies to go somewhere we may never have dreamt possible. We understand our assumptions and the way we do business will be challenged. Ultimately, it is a catalyst for growth for ourselves, our organizations, our audiences, and our community.

66

Above: Public Library of Charlotte & Mecklenberg County, ImaginOn: The Joe & Joan Martin Center

Right: McColl Family Theatre, ImaginOn: The Joe & Joan Martin Center

Auditorio Telmex, University of Guadalajara
Guadalajara, Jalisco, Mexico

Left and top: Auditorio Telmex, University of Guadalajara
Above: Lobby, Auditorio Telmex, University of Guadalajara

Center for the Performing Arts, Francis Marion University
Florence, South Carolina, USA

Left: Performance Hall, Center for the Performing Arts, Francis Marion University

Top: Center for the Performing Arts, Francis Marion University

Above: Lobby, Center for the Performing Arts, Francis Marion University

Doug Fitch 73

I started playing the violin when I was four and quickly noticed that it was fun to perform but not so fun to practice. At some point, my father—probably bored with the tedium of asking me to repeat things in order to improve the quality of my craft—came up with the brilliant notion of sticking a puppet on his hand, through whom he channeled his efforts to encourage my advancement. The performer in me was enchanted by my father's performance of the puppet and the rehearsal became a show! I was hooked and would do whatever the puppet told me.

I began making puppets for my father to use as my instructors and then just kept making them. When I was nine, I attended a college introductory course in the art of puppetry, taught by Frank Ballard at the University of Connecticut. At that time, Frank was the president of the Puppeteers of America Association and the chairman of the worldwide puppetry organization UNIMA (Union Internationale de la Marionnette), whose international convention arrived in my town the very next year, allowing me to become acquainted with some of the world's most accomplished practitioners of this curious art form.

Then my whole family got involved. We founded a puppet theater together, developing stories, making characters and scenery, writing music, and finding that among other fine attributes, our theater provided a wonderful excuse to get out of school, as we traveled around advancing the vision of our strange little parallel universe.

Left: The Institute of Contemporary Art
Following pages: Poss Family Mediatheque, The Institute of Contemporary Art

When it came time to apply to college, I brought a puppet to my Harvard interview. I credit my acceptance to this puppet's refreshing irreverence, which had the effect of making my own respect for the institution and desire to be accepted look more relaxed and genuine than it would have had I been forced to confront the interrogator "alone." Totally unplanned, it became a kind of talk show between two sides of my brain. I learned that my alter ego had a lot to say!

But it is not so surprising, when you think about it. Who is the audience for your inner voices? You can pray to God or unfold to a lover, but outwardly blathering one's inner banter is what crazy people do. Art, through its many mediums, offers a way to channel these inner voices through an "acceptable" other that serves to protect the boundaries of our selves while exploring territory we can only imagine, that is, the world beyond our only body—beyond our only mind.

Theater is the act of self-consciously reproducing the process of being human in the presence of others and thus is nothing if not collaborative. It involves reconfiguring the universe we think we know, with elements from the realm of imaginable possibilities. When we build a theater, we are constructing a vessel in which to simmer our collective subconscious. It is the pot in which we make stone soup from the stone of what we know, the water we are (mostly) made of, and the ingredients from our dreams. In this pot, we reduce the recognizable flavor of our own times to an essence of how it feels to be alive. We can taste the world as it might have been or could become. This enables us to better judge the soup we live in and make changes accordingly—seasoning to taste—as it were.

We try out visions of the world and try on alternate points of view. How do we feel and act when we live by a new set of rules or apply a different logic to what we have always done? What does it feel

It started with an invitation from Pinchus Zuckerman to do a version of *A Soldier's Tale* at Avery Fisher Hall with soloists from the New York Philharmonic. Because I had already staged a few productions with orchestras, (notably *Das Rheingold* with the Royal Stockholm Philharmonic and *L'Enfant et les Sortileges* with the National Symphony Orchestra), I knew how little time there would be to rehearse on stage, how severe the limitations would be on scenery and lighting (since the musicians need space to play and have to be able to see their music), and how, after everything was said and done, the unions could do everything possible to prevent any record of the work from being documented.

My response this time was to build a miniature theater like the kind they had in the Victorian times, where little drawings on sticks would move in and out with minimal action. This little magic box was filmed live and the world within it came to life above the heads of the musicians, projected on a large screen. I thought of my miniature theater as a "visual instrument" to be played alongside the musical instruments, uniting image and sound into a unique emergent quality. And I could control the lighting, the staging, take up minimal space, and actually have a record of the event! When I was invited to remount the production later in Canada at the National Arts Center, I realized there was a quality inherent to this kind of live animation that seemed to offer more potential for exploration.

like to shift our center of gravity and walk upside-down, or sing our sentences instead of speaking them? We re-contextualize ourselves by experimenting with different rationales, heightening or exaggerating elements from the world we live in, in order to draw our collective attention to a certain aspect of being human.

After forging a career involving designing houses and furniture, directing operas, professional brainstorming, drawing and painting, and making semi-functional objects of various sorts, I find I am coming back to the puppets of my childhood and, curiously, the world of music I was introduced to by practicing my violin. I have started developing a form of concert theater with miniature characters who perform live, onstage alongside symphony orchestras.

Above: Barbara Lee Family Foundation Theater, The Institute of Contemporary Art
Right: State Street Corporation Lobby, The Institute of Contemporary Art

Exploring that quality became a new business venture when producer/film-maker Edouard Getaz got involved and we started *Giants Are Small*. And once again, like in our family puppet theater days, I find myself working with my brother, Chris Fitch, who, in the meantime, became an artist of mechanical sculptures. Having invented new kinds of armatures for a stop-motion animation company, he brings an extraordinary level of artistic and technical skill to our new enterprise.

Our first production, *Peter and the Wolf*, opened at the Walt Disney Concert Hall and featured the Los Angeles Symphony. We wrote a prequel to the well-known story (underscored by excerpts from great classical music), which introduced Peter as a contemporary boy, living with his Russian grandfather who works as a gardener to a once-famous Los Angeles movie star (who has a cat), in a city whose unbridled growth encroached upon the territory of local wildlife (wolves) forcing them to trespass into man's habitat. Meanwhile, Peter is caught for having enabled 3,000 ducks to escape from a local foie gras factory where his kidnapped pet duck had been noticed. A little bird finds a kindred spirit in this courageous boy who saved a fellow feathered friend, befriends Peter and to a lesser and more conditional degree the duck, and the story unfolds from there.

Chris designed and constructed an elaborate miniature theater complete with an autonomous fly system, internal lighting, mechanical curtains, and a built-in camera dolly. With a team of creative individuals, we constructed miniature sets that could slide through the mechanical proscenium, blue-screen

backdrops, tiny little mechanical puppets, a shadow box, and many other story-telling devices. We were thus able to witness Peter sitting inside a LAPD car, being driven around a very real (pre-recorded) downtown Los Angeles; the cat reclining on a floating, inflatable, swimming-pool mattress; a ride through walls and through an impossible garden; and the duck surviving in the wolf's stomach by roasting marshmallows. In short, we can do things with our miniature world that would be very difficult to accomplish in a full-scale manner on stage. After *Peter and the Wolf*, we created a version of *Petrouchka* in which puppets were simply alive within the orchestra and the only proscenium was the one assumed by the camera's point of view.

The fact is, contemporary orchestras are being pressed to find innovative new ways to appeal to a contemporary audience. Playing the classics well is no longer enough to capture a younger, highly ocularcentric demographic. To do this, symphonies recognize that they can entice a new audience by introducing a visual component to the concert hall experience. We live in a visually demanding society and one no longer directly connected with the invention and evolution of the musical instruments that came to make up the standard classical orchestra. It is easy to take for granted the craftsmanship of an English horn from a distance of 50 feet. With the help of live-feed video projection and lighting, you can create a humble *gesamtkunstwerk*! This is exactly the kind of thing that the miniature theater technique is designed to respond to. It is a very malleable form of image-making, with which one can create imagery suited to all kinds of music, whether it is a story to be sung, a ballet to be danced, or a tone poem to be painted with light.

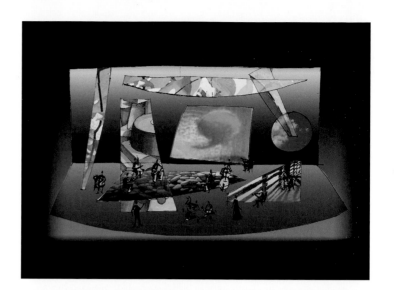

Now I am working on an opera called *Le Grand Macabre*, to be done with the New York Philharmonic under the direction of Alan Gilbert. My plan is to construct a miniature landscape that incorporates human-scale furnishings and runs along the front edge of the stage. Singers will interact with the landscapes, occasionally operating puppet versions of themselves, dunking them underwater, dismembering them, or doing whatever might otherwise be considered difficult (or dangerous), while singing. In this way, I am hoping to see the inner voices of these characters come to life as they are heard. What the camera captures will draw attention to the subtext of the story, which in this case concerns the absurdity of projecting doom and gloom on an unknowable future when life is a mystery best appreciated in its ephemeral, intangible, present tense— something to present yourself to and be present for.

Ever since our first game of peek-a-boo, we are engaged in this theatrical fascination of presenting ourselves. We reveal and conceal our gaze, using a mother's skirt, a wall, the surface of a table—whatever we find nearby, we use as a simple proscenium. These are theaters where the simple act of choosing to engage or disengage with an audience is played out. We make others believe we have the power to appear or disappear—to be or not to be.

It has always seemed to me that every piece of theater is best understood as a mindscape through which we are invited to see another "way." We can believe in it or not believe in it. It's just there—a box into which we pour our collective emotion and where, just like in a container of yogurt, culture is processed. We make theater to vitalize the intangible elements of life. We come to the theater to see ourselves practicing the art of being.

Top far left: Permanent Exhibit Gallery Space, The Institute of Contemporary Art

Top left: Putman Investments Plaza, The Institute of Contemporary Art

This page: Concepts for projection screens that inhabit the architecture of the theater, incorporating the audience into theater habitat

Left: Storytelling Festival, Council Chamber, George A. Purefoy Municipal Center

Above: Lobby, George A. Purefoy Municipal Center

Top: George A. Purefoy Municipal Center

Above: Custom fabrics and finishes, Council Chamber, George A. Purefoy Municipal Center

Right: Frisco City Council meeting, George A. Purefoy Municipal Center

Far right: Frisco Public Library, George A. Purefoy Municipal Center

Richard Buckley

There is a duality within me: the artistic and the non-artistic. In my life I am constantly negotiating a balance between these two forces. My personal partnership with these two driving energies informs how I perform in all circumstances. They are not contrarian, but require different attitudes and abilities when dealing with others. Having been in a leadership role most of my career, as a conductor, administrator, music director, and artistic director, I have had to continually adjust and reeducate myself as to how best to achieve results.

I grew up in an artistic family. Both parents were professional musicians, and they brought me into their world at a very young age. In my teens I investigated my own talents and ended up going through a number of steps before finding my path. Singer, pianist, actor, guitarist, bass trombonist, manager, conductor; bouncing between commercial and non-profit, opera, Broadway, symphony, and even ballet; and that was by the age of twenty-five along with a Masters degree. In living the above, the role model I had observed and experienced first hand was based on my benevolent dictator, monomaniac father (also a conductor), and a caring yet also driven diva mother.

Although I had great success in a very short period of time, the following 25 years were more about the development of relationships and partnerships. In the end, they make things happen that are much bigger than all of us collectively.

Left: Debra and Kevin Rollins Studio, Joe R. and Teresa Long Center for the Performing Arts

Following pages: Michael and Susan Dell Hall, Joe R. and Teresa Long Center for the Performing Arts

My artistic being, who has always been one to express itself in deed, not word, has had to learn to trust. If I do not find a way to work together, I usually experience results that are far from optimum. I continually seek to balance my individual assertiveness, with the more open stance of a collaboration or partnership.

When conducting, be it symphonic or operatic, working with instrumentalists or singers; as an administrator, working with staff and board; or as a community leader, working with all constituencies; one must lead, but also let go and let fate take its course. I pride myself in being knowledgeable and informed, usually organized, fast, detailed, and energized. Letting go of ego, excusing oneself from total responsibility, allowing partnering to occur, will more often arrive at a better result. This is important, and if done too late goals might not be achieved.

When a community decides to mount a major construction project such as a new arts complex, it is amazing that it ever gets built. I have just been a part of such a project, one that was on budget, on time, and artistically successful. It is remarkable to look at the different personalities that were in play, their styles, and their input toward the final end result. This project was made possible by the citizens and voters of Austin, Texas, who in 1998 approved two ballot measures: one to allow the lease of Palmer Auditorium, which was subsequently reconstructed to become the new Long Center, the other to assess a new rental-car tax to fund construction of the new Palmer Events Center and the park. The Long Center itself did not receive any public funds and the US$77 million project has been made possible by donations from more than 4,600 supporters of the arts in Austin, in amounts ranging from US$1 to $22 million.

I have been around other projects and theater renovations, but this was different because of my position as Artistic Director of Austin Lyric Opera. Dell Hall, the main performing facility of the Long Center is a multipurpose venue serving the Opera, Symphony, and Ballet. The project needed to address the theatrical needs of all three groups. The fundraising for the facility was from all of the arts patrons of the city. The individual arts organizations had their own expansionary programs in place, and the city was still reeling from a delayed reaction from the 2000 economic downturn. In addition, when I arrived in 2003 there was great project fatigue, and many millions had been spent on an architectural design that was tabled. People had become protective of their turf.

What has been achieved required many different types of personalities. The absolute need for dictators, benevolent or not, was at times required. Those same personalities had to be able to back off and be conciliatory. There were alliances created, trust, and distrust. There of course were strong egos, but how could there not be. In order to build this center, the community had to step up and identify itself as a city of the 21st century, one with 1.4 million inhabitants and no longer the small town of the 1960s. Neighborhood groups saw their part of town becoming more of the urban core. It required enormous community reeducation as to why this was important. Why a theater complex separate from the University of Texas helps define a city. But nothing happened without the partnership of all, working together to achieve the defined goal. Relationships between all stakeholders had to be forged. People with different backgrounds had to find a way to communicate. People had to let go of their individual prejudices and preconceived notions, and learn to communicate. What is a testament to all that participated is that the end product is more than what many believed could be accomplished.

Around the country, there are a number of other theater projects that are underway whose budgets are hundreds of million dollars more than ours was, but will they be that much better? No question the finishes will be different, the number of toys far greater, the lobby space more, but the soul of a theater is not made up of those things. Hopefully their process will achieve both its architectural vision and its city's cultural identity. The individual soul of a theater is the end result of all the relationships and partnerships that created it. That is why a theater is not just a building, and it is in its own right an individual piece of art. We the artists then perform our art in partnership with it.

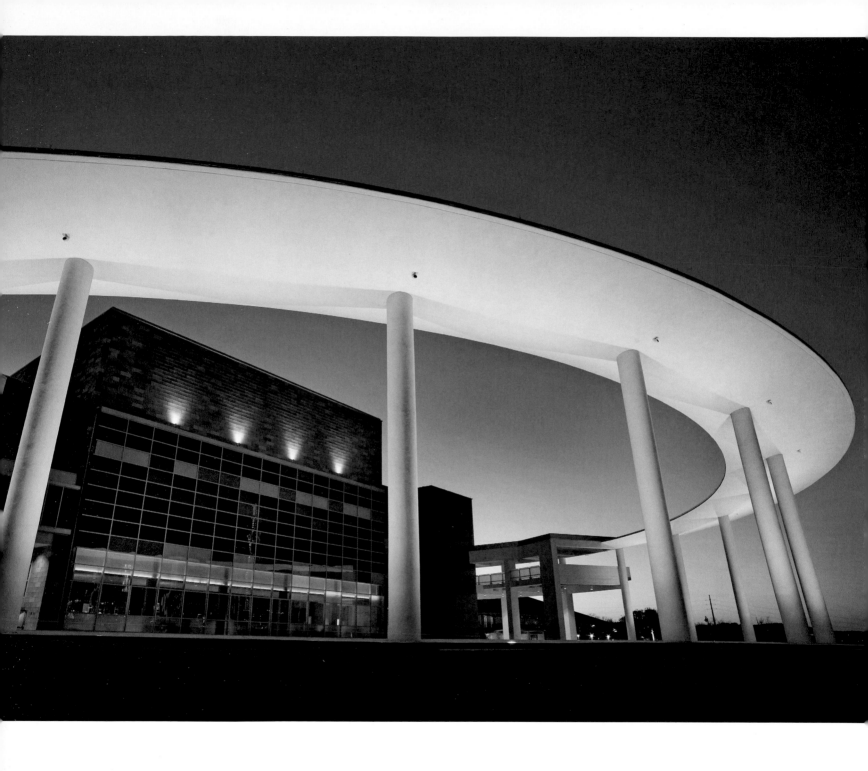

Above: Eva and Marvin Womack Courtyard, Joe R. and Teresa Long Center for the Performing Arts

Left: Music Hall, Kansas City Music Hall
Top: Interior cross section, Kansas City Music Hall
Above: Lobby extension rendering, Kansas City Music Hall

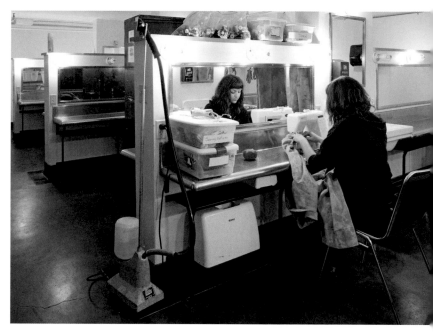

Left: Kansas City Music Hall

Top: Lobby, Kansas City Music Hall

Above: Support spaces, Kansas City Music Hall

Jack Finlaw

95

During the late 1990s, Denver civic leaders and performing arts organizations began urging the City's political leaders to renovate the City's 90-year-old municipal auditorium, which was being used for Colorado Ballet productions and occasional family-oriented touring shows. Newton Auditorium was shabby in the extreme and had fire and other safety code violations; the venue also did not accommodate people with disabilities. The City's Theatres and Arenas Division worked for about five years to put together public funding to renovate the facility. Because Denver had a long history of constructing and renovating its public assembly facilities primarily with public monies, no real effort was made to create a public–private partnership for this project.

At this time the local opera company, Opera Colorado, was alternately performing in the City's symphony hall and Broadway roadhouse. Leaders of this organization, of which I was a member, lobbied city officials to create a new state-of-the-art opera house inside the old Newton Auditorium. Design work was done for a US$75-million renovation project that would build an opera house inside the existing walls of the historic municipal auditorium. This resulted in a US$500,000 campaign, funded by Opera Colorado board members, to convince voters to approve a US$25-million general obligation bond; in November 2002 the people of Denver voted, with 68 percent approving the bond. The proceeds from the US$25-million general obligation bond, US$45 million in certificates of participation (a quasi-debt instrument sold by the City to

Left: Susan Brotman Auditorium, Marion Oliver McCaw Hall at Seattle Center

investors in a public offering), US$5 million from the seat tax reserve fund (a fund that exists because all patrons of the performing arts in Denver-owned venues pay an admission tax equal to 10 percent of the ticket price), and approximately US$2 million of Theatres and Arenas' capital improvement budget (also funded by the seat tax) made up the US$75-million construction budget.

At the outset, no private funding was budgeted. The opera house project began in May 2003, the same month that a new mayor was elected. Mayor John Hickenlooper appointed me to be the Director of Theatres and Arenas in September 2003 and I took over management of the project and immediately began private fundraising efforts in order to increase its size and scope, the desire for which came from Theatres and Arenas and several other civic and performing arts organizations. Though Opera Colorado leaders, in particular, lobbied city officials to build a state-of-the-art opera house, both the opera company and Colorado Ballet were consulted throughout the planning and design phases of the Newton Auditorium renovation. Building a venue that met all of the acoustical, visual, and technical needs of both organizations was paramount.

Above: Kreielsheimer Promenade, Marion Oliver McCaw Hall at Seattle Center

Top right: Kreielsheimer Promenade, Lighting Artist, Leni Schwendinger, Marion Oliver McCaw Hall at Seattle Center

Right: Grand Lobby, Sculpture by Sarah Sze, Marion Oliver McCaw Hall at Seattle Center

We received a US$7-million gift that brought with it the naming rights to the new opera house, a US$2-million gift, and approximately US$5 million in additional gifts, primarily from Opera Colorado board members who wanted to fund the build-out of spaces in the auditorium that could not be completed with the public monies available. Theatres and Arenas carried out the private fundraising for the project; this was a very difficult and time-consuming process, especially because we had no support staff for fundraising.

Opera Colorado and Colorado Ballet were not asked to undertake major fundraising efforts for the construction of the Ellie Caulkins Opera House because neither was slated to be the primary tenant of the new venue. Both operate on a partial-year performance schedule, and while the facility was certainly intended to serve as a world-class opera house and become the permanent home of both the opera and ballet companies, the aim had always been to create a multiple-use venue that could also house touring Broadway productions and a diverse array of performances and events. When it became clear that the City's commitment of US$75 million would not be enough to complete every component of the new facility, several patrons of both Opera Colorado and Colorado Ballet stepped up to contribute private donations and pledges.

Theatres and Arenas is now tasked with renovating Boettcher Concert Hall, a 30-year-old symphony hall that suffers from inconsistent acoustics and a lack of adequate musician, business, and public support spaces and amenities. The concert hall project is vastly different from the renovation of the municipal auditorium in that the Colorado Symphony Orchestra (CSO), the main tenant of the hall, offered from the beginning to seek private monies for a new symphony center and donate it to the City. With a recent election approving another general obligation bond, we have US$60 million of public monies and US$30 million of private monies raised by the CSO.

The proposed renovation of Boettcher Concert Hall fell closely on the heels of the City's sizeable financial commitment in rebuilding the Newton Auditorium, presenting Theatres and Arenas with a more complex funding challenge. With construction at the auditorium just completed in 2005, not enough time had passed for the City to recoup its investment, therefore further limiting the available funds for a possible Boettcher overhaul. This challenge was recognized from the onset and it was understood that the only way to fund another large-scale project at a city-owned venue was to call on the building's primary tenant for assistance in finding funds. The Colorado Symphony Orchestra has been the primary tenant of Boettcher Concert Hall for 30 years, and the planned improvements and expansion would unequivocally sustain the longevity of the organization within the community. With a commitment of at least US$30 million in private funding, the CSO will in effect become a one-third owner of the renovated facility.

The partnerships we cultivated for the renovation and expansion of these two venues helped fund the added costs and grow the scope of the projects. Bringing private dollars to the table adds another layer to the building of these venues as the input of donors must be considered and respected. Because Theatres and Arenas did all of the fundraising internally for the opera house project, we retained total control of the renovation. In the case of the Boettcher Concert Hall project, the symphony expects to have a much greater say in the choice of acoustician, architect, and contractor and final say on the design of the hall.

The role the CSO will play in the future of the symphony hall expansion is of a much broader scope than that of the organizations involved in the renovation of the Newton Auditorium. Since Boettcher Concert Hall is a purpose-built facility that will continue to primarily serve the efforts of the CSO and its programming, educational, community outreach, and administrative support goals, the organization has had a tremendous impact on the initial phases of the renovation, and will continue to do so through the completion of the project. For this reason, coupled with the significant amount of money the tenant organization has committed to the project, the City's relationship with the CSO throughout this endeavor will be one of total partnership. Even after construction has been completed and the doors of the new symphony hall have been opened to the public, the city and the CSO will continue to work together in a unique landlord-tenant capacity that allows for cooperative management of facility.

Roe Green Center,
Kent State University
Kent, Ohio, USA

Left: Black Box theater, Roe Green Center, Kent State University
Top: Roe Green Center, Kent State University
Above: Lobby, Roe Green Center, Kent State University

Top: Tokyo International Forum
Above: Hall C, Tokyo International Forum
Top right and right: Glass Hall, Tokyo International Forum
Far right: Hall A, Tokyo International Forum

Benjamin & Marion Schuster Performing Arts Center
Dayton, Ohio, USA

Neal Gittelman

103

For years I believed the old saw that no multipurpose hall could function as a true concert hall. That old saw was proven wrong once and for all in the Mead Theatre of Dayton's Benjamin and Marian Schuster Performing Arts Center. But why construct a multipurpose hall for Dayton in the first place? Because it was not within the community's resources to have separate, dedicated venues for symphony, opera, Broadway, and dance. If Dayton was going to get a new, state-of-the-art facility it would have to be a multipurpose hall. And it would have to be a multipurpose hall that could also function as a true concert hall, regardless of the old saw.

The Schuster Center succeeded because of the partnerships formed. A group of local business leaders stepped up and bought a long-vacant block in downtown with the express purpose of developing a new performing arts center. The leaders of the major arts groups—the Dayton Philharmonic Orchestra, Dayton Opera, Dayton Ballet, and the Victoria Theatre Association (our local Broadway presenter)—partnered to make their acoustical and theatrical requirements clear and explicit, and spoke with one unified voice. A comprehensive fundraising effort generated the necessary funds, comprising local donors both large and small, two major appropriations from the Ohio State Legislature, support from city and county government, and federal funds provided through our regional mass transit authority. The architects, acousticians, and theater designers partnered to create a facility that met the performers'

Left: Mead Theater, Benjamin & Marion Schuster Performing Arts Center

requirements with beauty, elegance, and efficiency. The project managers kept everyone on task. Hundreds of workers partnered to execute the design on time, on budget, and on target. And a crackerjack house crew partnered with performers, playing the hall's equipment and adjustable features like Heifetz on a Strad, making everyone sound and look their best.

The result is a theater that serves all its users well. For the Victoria Theatre Association it is a first-class venue for touring Broadway shows. For Dayton Ballet it is a magnificent showcase for the dancers. For Dayton Opera it's a great opera house where words can be understood and the pit never overpowers the stage. And best of all for me and my colleagues in the Dayton Philharmonic Orchestra, it's truly a world-class concert hall, with an amazing combination of warmth and

clarity that flatters the orchestra, thrills the audience, and flabbergasts our guest artists.

The Mead Theatre's greatest asset is its flexibility. In addition to providing an appropriate acoustical environment for each different user, it can adapt to each of the many types of performances the Dayton Philharmonic presents: traditional full orchestra and chorus-plus-orchestra repertoire in the full-depth shell; chamber orchestra repertoire in a shallower shell; pops repertoire with heavily amplified guest artists and miked orchestra; a mix of acoustical orchestra with "quieter" pops guests. We have even closed off the proscenium opening entirely for chamber music and solo piano recitals. In every case we have been able to fine-tune the acoustics of the hall to match the music.

Five years in, the Schuster Center runs smoothly and efficiently. The facility is owned and managed by the Victoria Theatre Association, which judiciously balances its dual function as building landlord and theatrical presenter. Resident groups are not ousted from their dates in the building in order to accommodate touring shows. While this policy is not carved in stone, it is the result of a strong commitment on the part of the Victoria's senior staff and Board of Directors to honor the scheduling needs of the local performing groups that use the Schuster Center. If there is a challenge ahead, it will be to make that enlightened policy an explicit part of the Center's "DNA," so that tradition will continue even when new faces are on the scene.

The Mead Theatre has done nothing less than revolutionize the arts in Dayton and made our town a destination for music, dance, and theater patrons throughout Southwest Ohio. It is a great hall, and a perfect example of the power of creative partnerships.

Top left: Dayton Philharmonic Orchestra, Benjamin & Marion Schuster Performing Arts Center

Above: Wintergarden, Benjamin & Marion Schuster Performing Arts Center

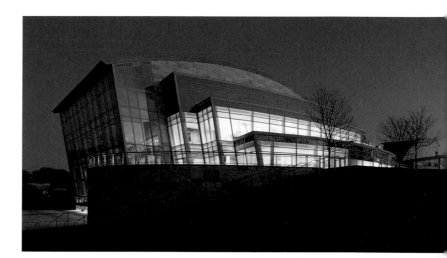

Left and above: Concert Hall, The Music Center at Strathmore
Top: The Music Center at Strathmore

Plácido Domingo

It is my good fortune to work in three different capacities in my chosen profession—as a singer, conductor, and general director of two opera companies, the Washington National Opera and the Los Angeles Opera. Thus I experience a performance space from the stage, from the pit, from the auditorium itself, from behind the scenes, and even from the administrative offices. Within recent times, I witnessed the creation of two magnificent new halls in the United States: by singing at the opening of the new Renée and Henry Segerstrom Concert Hall in Orange County, California and by being an attendant at several concerts in the Walt Disney Concert Hall, the new home of the Los Angeles Philharmonic. Both are outstanding examples of what a boon new halls can be for the performer as well as for the public, as is also the new opera house in Valencia, Spain, where I sang recently. I think that congratulations are in order to all who created these new spaces for music, as I am also sure that there are many other such shining examples here and abroad, like the new opera houses in Copenhagen and Oslo. Yet not everywhere the performer and the public are so fortunate.

As a singer and conductor I am of course tremendously concerned about acoustics. By the same token I have come to recognize that in a number of cases acoustics have, to a degree, obliterated other concerns; especially the concern for aesthetics. Having not only performed in almost every music-loving country in the world but also having been a listener to other performing artists, I have often sat in an auditorium that had decent-to-good acoustics but was depressingly dreary. To my

Left: Paint shop, Oslo Opera House

mind there is no excuse for this because attending any kind of performance should be a joyous and festive occasion. There is one famous hall, which shall remain nameless, where I am always tempted to say that a bright new paint job and brighter lighting would even improve the "perception" of the acoustics. Aesthetics are important to all our senses and therefore it is a fallacy to sacrifice the eye-appeal in order to achieve the best possible sound. History has shown that a good auditorium can have glorious sound and at the same time be architecturally appealing. There are many such examples like the Musiekverein in Vienna; the Opera House in Wiesbaden, Germany; Carnegie

Hall in New York City; Teatro Colon in Buenos Aires; and the Metropolitan Opera at Lincoln Center in New York City to mention a mere few. By the way, the Metropolitan is a good example of what I mentioned above. When it opened on September 16, 1966, all the fronts of the different tiers featured a lot of white paint. The impression was of unrest and confusion. The aesthetic sense of the wonderful Met patron, the late Sybil Harrington, must have been disturbed by this because—so I have been told—at her instance and with her financial largesse, a great deal of the auditorium was soon repainted to feature exclusively the reddish maroon which it has to this day.

Every time I attend a Met performance, I marvel not only at the acoustics, but also at the calming festivity of the auditorium.

For the performer the backstage is of great importance. Lack of spacious and well-equipped dressing rooms is demoralizing and robs the performer of that ultimate feeling of joyous adventure in performing. I know, among new opera houses, examples where the backstage area is not only luxuriously large for storing scenery, but where little thought was given to the comfort of the performer, because the main dressing rooms are not only cramped but are on different levels from the stage.

At such places one stands waiting seemingly hours for the elevator to finally come and take one to the stage level. When one stands at last in the wings to go out on stage, one has become needlessly tense.

No architect can be faulted when the management of the company denies the importance of scenery to bounce the voice out into the auditorium or when a scenic designer is unaware

Left: Foyer, Oslo Opera House
Above: Main auditorium, Oslo Opera House

that a lot of cloth in the scenery—especially velvet—absorbs too much sound. There is an amusing story that was told to me by the tour manager of the late famous French coloratura Lily Pons. It seems that she was giving a recital in a high school gymnasium that had been converted into a makeshift auditorium. As she walked out on the stage, she noticed that it was created entirely by velvet drapes. Before singing a single note, she marched off the stage and exclaimed to the stage manager, "Zee velvet draperies must go, or I weel not sing!" The poor man was trying to argue with her but she was adamant. Just as she was walking out in her stunning concert gown, the audience started to laugh and applaud. The last velvet hanging had fallen to the floor and, in doing so, had revealed a sign that read, with an arrow pointing off stage, "To the lavatories." It is to the credit of her performance that after the initial hilarity, she had the audience in the palms of her hands for the rest of the evening.

Rehearsal spaces are also of real importance because this is where the groundwork for the ultimate performance is laid. Two outstanding examples that come to mind are the orchestra rehearsal rooms at both the Gran Teatre del Liceu in Barcelona and the Teatro Real in Madrid. In both places, the orchestra rehearsal rooms take place in spaces with an abundance of windows through which one has a panoramic view of practically the entire city. The mood this creates is one of exhilaration.

I have performed in both Lincoln Center opera houses; first at the State Theater with the New York City Opera, and then, for the past 39 years, at the Metropolitan. I have often gone to the administrative offices of both companies and my reaction to those meetings has been decidedly different. The offices at the State Theater are depressing, because they are in the subterranean level of the building and have no windows. Every time I came away from such a meeting I felt not only depressed but also claustrophobic. The opposite was true at the Met, where practically every office has windows and is pleasingly furnished. As an administrator in both Los Angeles and Washington, I have the luxury of a cheerful office, as have most of the other staff members.

Right: Main auditorium, Oslo Opera House

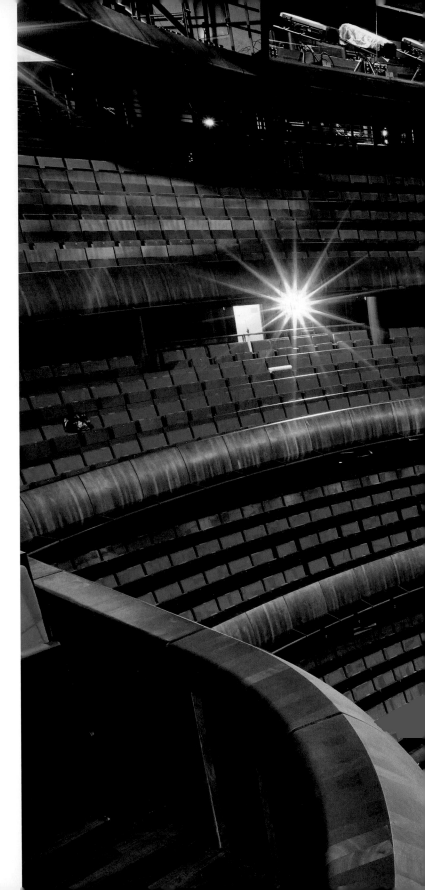

Much has been written about acoustics and the general consensus is that even with our advanced understanding of the "meaning" of acoustics, we still cannot call it a real science. Yes, we know that the shape of the auditorium is important to the sound; that wood is the ideal paneling for the walls; that the old rococo ornamentations in the auditoriums built in past centuries did much for the ideal dissemination of the sound—something we are trying to achieve today in modern architecture through changeable acoustical baffles; and that the majority of the materials used in a hall need to age. The most striking example of this is Argentina's Teatro Colon. It was originally built not only for music and dance presentations but also for political rallies. As a matter of fact, it was christened by a series of such rallies, with politicians trying to make speeches. Being the pre-microphone era, those orators had a tough time projecting their voices. They certainly did not project to the far away corners of the balconies. The upshot was that the theater was deemed hopeless and sealed up for more than a year. In that year, with a climate ranging from extreme summer heat to cold winters, the wood in the theater apparently aged drastically. When it was re-opened (for what function I do not know), the people discovered that even a whisper could be heard in the upper-most tiers. As a singer I can tell you that it is a rare joy to perform in that house.

Even paint must age, something that became apparent to some of us performers after the fairly recent renovation of Carnegie Hall. Thank heaven that now it has that old acoustical quality again that made it originally so famous. That we have made tremendous strides in building new spaces where classical music can flourish is something all of us rejoice in. That there is still room for further improvements gives us even greater confidence that the Arts can flourish as never before.

115

Left: Oslo Opera House

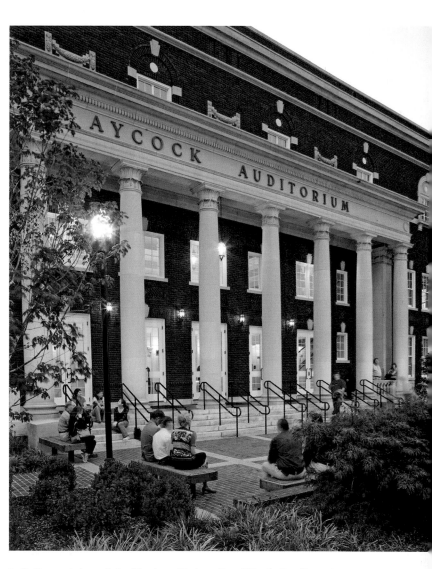

Left: Concert, Aycock Auditorium, University of North Carolina at Greensboro

Above: Restored 1927 Aycock Auditorium, University of North Carolina at Greensboro

Top: Graduation ceremonies circa 1930, Aycock Auditorium, University of North Carolina at Greensboro

Above: Interior circa 1950, Aycock Auditorium, University of North Carolina at Greensboro

Right: Aycock Auditorium, University of North Carolina at Greensboro

Far right: Lobby, Aycock Auditorium, University of North Carolina at Greensboro

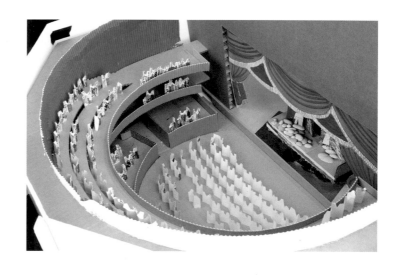

Top far left: Center for the Arts, New Mexico State University
Top left: Theater, Center for the Arts, New Mexico State University
Left: Center for the Arts, New Mexico State University
Above: Theater model, Center for the Arts, New Mexico State University

George Austin

Through renovation and significant expansion of the former Madison Civic Center, the new Overture Center for the Arts is a unique destination of seven performance venues, four art galleries, and the Madison Museum of Contemporary Art, located just one block from the State Capitol in Madison, Wisconsin. At 400,000 square feet, the performing and visual arts center occupies a full city block and anchors a vibrant cultural arts district in the heart of the city. Its completion in 2006 accelerated the revitalization of this central area. Developed in partnership with the City of Madison and local arts organizations, Overture Center was entirely funded by a single gift of US$210 million by local citizen W. Jerome Frautschi. Owned by the private non-profit Overture Development Corporation, the facility is operated by the public Madison Cultural Arts District.

Overture Center for the Arts is the product of a public–private collaboration. Without the intricate cooperation among the arts community, the City, and the donor, the project could never have been realized. To initiate the planning process, a 48-member advisory council was formed of community leaders, artists, and cultural arts organizations to identify and prioritize the space, needs, and priorities that should be addressed with the Frautschi gift. Following technical studies by the Overture planning team composed of the owner, architect, acoustician, theater planner, and operations expert, town hall meetings were held across the community. Attended by more than 400 citizens and televised locally, the forums provided a rich

Left: The Playhouse, Overture Center for the Arts

dialogue about the hopes, dreams, and concerns regarding the project. From this community participation, a public vision emerged for the role of the arts in the City's central area. A committed team of Overture planners was then able to shape the big idea and bold vision of the donor with the community desire for a wide variety of spaces available for the performing and visual arts.

The result is an exceptional urban infill project that is a resourceful use of land and an enhancement of the built environment. The Overture Center for the Arts is located in downtown Madison on a 2.5-acre site formerly occupied by the Madison Civic Center. The project incorporated the historic elements of the Madison Civic Center into the new project, and reused building and theater equipment from the center as part of the new project. The Madison Civic Center opened in 1980 and served as the home to many local groups including the Madison Symphony Orchestra, Madison Opera, Madison Repertory Theatre, and Madison Art Center. By the mid-1990s it was becoming clear that the Madison Civic Center was increasingly inadequate in its ability to meet the needs of the

local arts organizations. This situation led to two community funded studies: the first conducted in 1996, detailed the rising space needs faced by Madison's arts organizations, and the second in 1997 and 1998, recommended expansion of the Civic Center. Shortly thereafter, in July of 1998, W. Jerome Frautschi, a retired Madison businessman and lifelong Dane County resident, announced his intent to give a major gift for the renovation and expansion of the arts facilities in downtown Madison.

The gift was made in conjunction with the City of Madison's Downtown 2000 Plan, which called for cultural facilities and activities to fulfill a larger role in the City's downtown revitalization strategy and become an important element in the creation of a healthy central city. Downtown 2000 laid the groundwork for the increased investment in cultural arts activities as a focus for the central business district. Frautschi's gift, which enabled an expansion of the municipally owned Madison Civic Center, was the catalyst of an elaborate public–private effort. Achieving a viable plan required significant cooperation between the private and public partners in all phases of the project.

Internationally recognized architect Cesar Pelli infused the project with an innovative design. Given a complex set of objectives and many design challenges, Pelli blended new with old, integrating the new 2,250-seat Overture Hall with the previous 350-seat Playhouse and the former 1,000-seat Oscar Mayer Theatre, designed by Rapp and Rapp as a grand movie palace in 1927. Performance and visual arts facilities interconnect in one complex, creating large and small, formal and informal spaces, maintaining the urban design qualities of the State Street shopping district, and accommodating the greater bulk of a large performance hall while keeping a pedestrian-friendly environment. Further, he designed a building that does not compete with Madison's architectural icon, the State Capitol, one block from the site.

Overture Center for the Arts has the benefit of the vibrant city around it. As noted urban writer and activist Jane Jacobs, who championed new, community-based approaches to planning for more than 40 years, said during the Lincoln Center debate in New York City in 1958, "The natural neighbors of halls are

restaurants, bars, florist shops, studios, music shops, all sorts of interesting places." State Street and Madison's central business district fit that prescription perfectly. Overture Center is a new contributor to Madison's central retail artery, forming a direct relationship with the activities already in place around the center. The opening nine-day festival in September 2004 drew over 60,000 attendees. For the 2006–07 season, the first full year of operation for the completed facility, attendance at community and education programming at Overture Center was 126,777 compared to 86,021 in the 2003–04 season, the last year of operation at the former Madison Civic Center, a 47 percent increase in attendance. Overture Center's ticketed events saw an even greater increase in attendance of 70 percent over the same period.

Today, people seek places that are unique and authentic. A community's livability is based on many factors, but it is a community's cultural resources that make it distinct. Overture Center is a catalyst that is unleashing Madison's and Dane County's cultural resources. As a result, opportunities have been created for our fellow citizens to share experiences of art, music, dance, and to engage each other in our daily lives that further tie us together in a shared economic and social future. In the end, that is the most important measure of the project.

Left: Rotunda Stage, Overture Center for the Arts
Above: Lobby overlooking Rotunda Stage, Overture Center for the Arts
Following pages: Overture Hall, Overture Center for the Arts

Far left, left, above: Nancy Lee and Perry R. Bass Performance Hall

Frank Turner

The Plano Courtyard Theater and Cox Building are a highly successful community theater and educational complex in historic downtown Plano, Texas. This two-phase, US$11-million adaptive reuse project created a vibrant cultural asset that strengthened community partnerships and advanced downtown's renaissance. The project demonstrates that landmark preservation and adaptive reuse are effective tools in enriching suburban cities, in addition to their role in core urban areas.

Plano is a nationally recognized, rapidly growing suburb. Expanding from a population of 3,500 in 1960 to more than 260,000 today, the city is a leading American "Boomburg." Evidence of Plano's farm town genesis is scarce, a fact that may contribute to the growing public interest in preserving historic landmarks and revitalizing the city's small downtown. The Cox Building (formerly Cox School) and its adjacent gymnasium, located on the edge of downtown, are the city's oldest public buildings. Built in the 1920s and 1930s respectively, the buildings proudly served generations of Plano students. When suburbanization demanded modern schools, the aging buildings were reoccupied with administrative and ancillary uses. By the late 1990s, the obsolete, deteriorating buildings were in limited use. The beauty and the integrity of their original design were lost through numerous piecemeal modifications; yet, the buildings were local landmarks and they occupied a strategic downtown location within a short walk of the planned Dallas

Far left: Plano Courtyard Theater
Top left: Lobby balcony, Plano Courtyard Theater
Left: Wedding in lobby, Plano Courtyard Theater

Area Rapid Transit (DART) light rail station. Restoring the buildings was important to downtown's continued rebirth, but it depended on finding a suitable use that would attract community support.

The Cox Building and gymnasium held great promise for meeting Plano's growing need for arts and cultural facilities. The city of Plano and the Plano Independent School District joined as partners in 1999 to transform the 22,000-square-foot gymnasium into the Plano Courtyard Theater. Nearly US$6.5 million was committed to the theater project, including substantial private gifts. Public funding came primarily from a tax increment finance district, in which Collin County and Collin College joined the city and school district as contributors of ad

valorem tax growth. Hardy Holzman Pfeiffer Associates (HHPA) led the project design team with guidance from community art organizations, nearby residents, and downtown merchants throughout design and construction.

Although the gymnasium was structurally sound, adapting the building to its new use required gutting it so only the exterior building shell remained. Now reconstructed, the theater chamber (seating and stage) occupies space originally used for athletic events. A balcony surrounds the floor level seating and creates the intimate courtyard feel for which the theater is named. The

Above: Plano Courtyard Theater
Right: Lobby, Plano Courtyard Theater

resulting 325-seat, flexible format theater is well suited to a wide variety of artistic uses. Space once used for locker rooms and classrooms is today a gracious, oversized lobby and back-of-house facilities. The interior's design and finish are modern, but with elements reminiscent of the building's past. HHPA playfully selected materials, including cattle-trailer metal siding, as homage to the city's agrarian past. The front lobby's wooden floor reminds visitors that the space was once a gym. The restored exterior of the Courtyard Theater, including its new barrel roof, conforms to the building's original design by architect Hoke Smith. The theater opened in April 2002 to praise for its design and successful preservation of an important landmark. Community art organizations appreciated the much-needed theatrical venue and the restored building instantly reconnected to the community like the return of an old friend with a new job. Its intimate and adaptive qualities provide performers and patrons an exceptional environment for experiencing theatrical, dance, and musical performances. The theater lobby also serves as an art gallery and is frequently used for receptions, dinners, and meetings.

The success of the Courtyard Theater immediately led community leaders to discuss the future of the adjacent three-story Cox Building. The two buildings are inseparable parts of the same community landmark. The underutilized Cox Building was physically declining, but restoration and reuse again depended on functional and economic considerations. Enlarging on their previous successful partnership, the city, school district, and other taxing jurisdictions decided in 2004 to allocate US$4.6 million from the tax increment finance district for restoration of the building. Good, Fulton and Farrell Architects (GFF) was selected to head the design team and community stakeholders were core partners in the process of design and construction oversight.

The Cox Building reopened in January 2006. Refining a concept initially developed by HHPA, GFF added a new lobby, stairway, and elevator tower on the building's south side to provide easy access to all levels, including the new 100-seat black-box theater. The new lobby and an arcade join the Cox Building to the Courtyard Theater, both functionally and aesthetically.

The addition complements the Cox Building's exterior, but is easily distinguished from the original structure. The new interior is contemporary, except for the vintage design of the entrance hall and a reconstructed "historic" classroom. The exterior of the building is restored to its original 1924 appearance as designed by W.A. Tackett. In 2007, the Cox Building and Courtyard Theater were added to the Texas Register of Historic Places and they received the Greater Dallas Planning Council's Project Award for Urban Design.

Restoration and reuse of the two buildings was truly a single project spanning nearly 10 years of planning and construction. It was made possible by the partnership of the city of Plano, the Plano Independent School District, Collin County, and Collin College—a remarkably rare occurrence of a common goal receiving tax support from four local governmental bodies. Equally important to the project's success were the backing and contributions provided by more than a dozen local not-for-profit arts organizations, the Plano Heritage Commission, neighborhood residents, local business leaders, and the Plano Arts and Cultural Endowment (PACE). To date, PACE has contributed more than US$216,000 to enhance the Courtyard Theater and Cox Building. In 2007, the combined facilities showcased more than 250 events, including live theater, concerts, dance, community meetings, and educational programs conducted by scores of community-based organizations. Additionally, the restored landmark

attracts numerous visitors, alumnae and students learning about the community's heritage.

Situated on the western edge of downtown Plano, the Courtyard Theater and Cox Building are stimulating reinvestment in downtown and surrounding neighborhoods. The project cemented confidence in the area's future and increased developer and consumer activity. Two new residential projects are under construction within 1,000 feet of the Courtyard Theater and will add more than 200 "for sale" units to downtown's housing inventory. The Courtyard Theater and Cox Building are an activity center and focal point unifying downtown, Haggard Park and adjacent neighborhoods. They enrich the area and contribute to creating a sustainable urban environment.

Arriving by DART to the Downtown Plano Station, you immediately sense that you are in a special place. It is a place tied to its heritage, yet uniquely fresh and exciting—a place to meet, talk, stroll, sit on a bench, see a play, eat, shop, and live. Downtown Plano's unique mix of old and new, variety of architectural styles, and diversity of use creates an authentic wholeness made even more special by theater and the arts.

Left and above left: Plano Courtyard Theater
Above: Restored 1927 Cox Gymnasium, Plano Courtyard Theater

The New York Times Center
New York, New York, USA

Left and above: The Times Center Stage, The New York Times Center

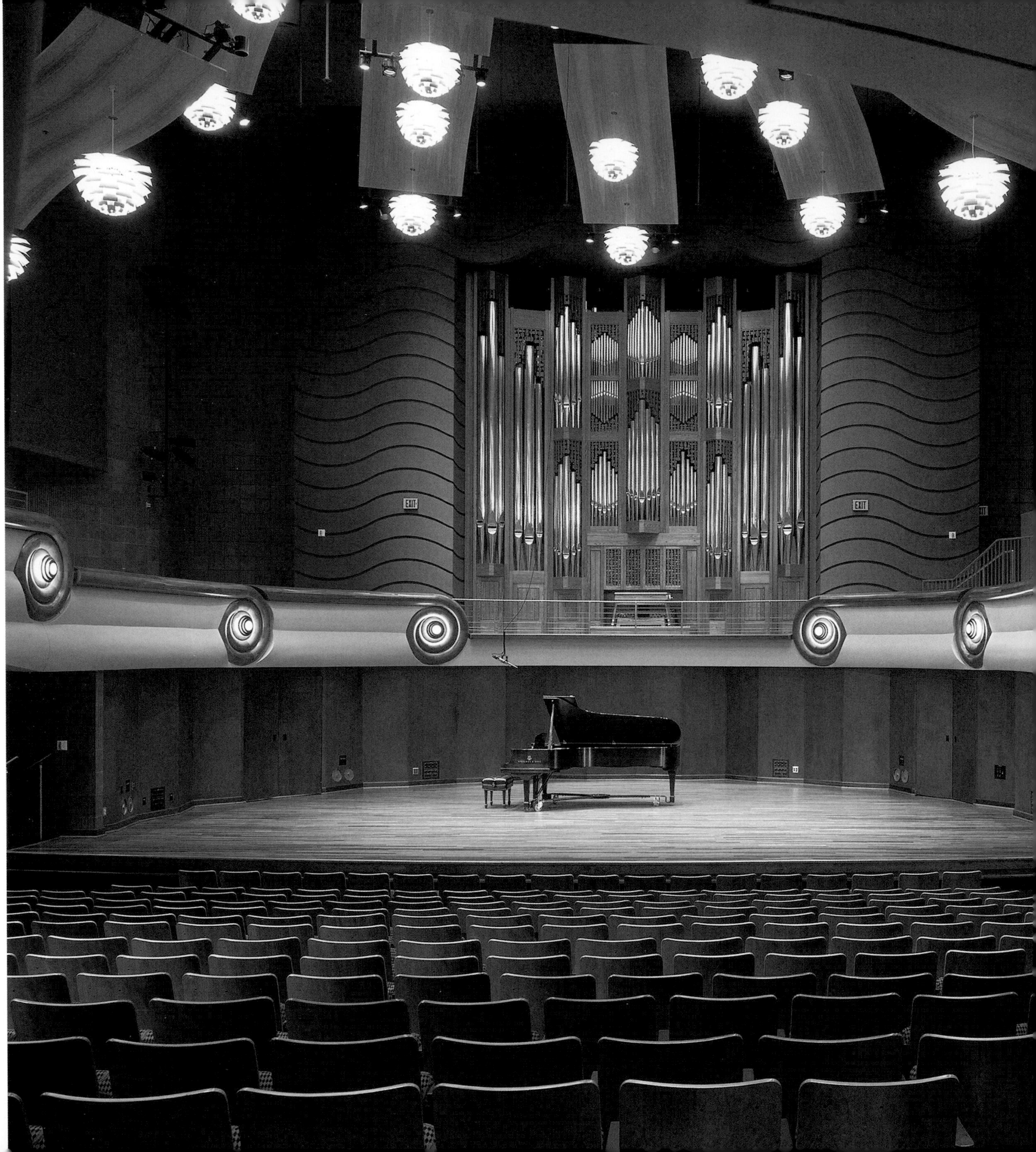

James Baudoin

139

Communities across America are facing greater challenges now than ever before in the planning and construction of new performing arts centers. Due to increasing costs associated with this complex building type, the traditional municipal approach that relied specifically on allocating public bond dollars has evolved into public partnerships with the private sector. Success comes with private donors and government officials working in tandem.

Rises in general construction costs plus changes in expectations by both owners and designers are requiring that evermore funding sources be identified. A key development has been a significant escalation in costs related to materials, design and labor, as well as due to requirements to ensure compliance with government codes. Another series of issues is connected to the increasing sophistication of theatrical systems demanded to meet production power, lighting and sound expectations for both concert and theater activities.

Creation of successful new performing arts center projects is now a matter of finding the right mix of community leaders from the public and private sectors. Good leadership enables projects to secure necessary funding and empowers partners to formulate and use appropriate sequences of activities during pre-opening processes.

In recent decades, innovative ideas using successful public–private partnerships have been developed to support the rising costs of new performing arts center projects. The Portland

Left: Legacy Hall, RiverCenter for the Performing Arts

Performing Arts Center in Oregon, the RiverCenter in Georgia and the Arts of Collin County in Texas each utilized different approaches to fund construction with a varied mix of public–private initiatives. These projects faced major obstacles before moving forward but ultimately succeeded with strong leadership and broad-based community support.

An Oregon Project in the 1980s

Portland's effort began with the private sector demonstrating its commitment.

"The difference in Portland," according to Pat Harrington, founding Executive Director of the Portland Center for the Performing Arts, "was that the community was transitioning from a small town to a big city. The arts community was maturing and the need for more performing arts facilities was evident." A public bond measure in 1981 and a private sector donor committing US$3 million served as the motivator for this public–private partnership, which ultimately generated more government dollars and added additional private gifts down the road. "Public and private leadership recognized the value of cultural growth in impacting economic development," stated Harrington.

A private sector group in Portland was empowered to raise the balance needed for the US$42-million goal. Additionally, on achievement of the goal by the private campaign, public dollars were added by the sale of an old police building property with

proceeds provided to the performing arts center project. City support later came from using excess bond proceeds from recent municipal projects. Harrington noted: "While the private sector donor stepping forward was the impetuous for the project, the effort really did not move forward until a public vote made the project real."

Success did not happen overnight: as with most projects it developed over a period of years. "The mantra of the day to overcome was—We Don't Need It, We Can't Afford It and We Will Never Accomplish It—and that's what we had to overcome," said Harrington.

Harrington goes on to explain, "We unleashed our effort in the way that was appropriate for Portland at the time, which was to get the arts community to go door to door. There was no city money to start a campaign. Instead community meetings built a groundswell of grass-roots support. We kept momentum by raising money and using the major constituent arts organizations and volunteers to help keep the effort alive."

The Oregon Symphony rehearsed for years in an undersized space above the civic auditorium. Its leadership aggressively campaigned for renovating the historic Paramount into a venue now named the Arlene Schnitzer Concert Hall. Two existing Portland groups, the New Rose and Storefront theatre companies, publicly asserted the need for the new legitimate theater spaces.

Portland's local government responded to the need for something more than its aging 3,000-seat civic auditorium. It was the mayor who initiated the private sector committee. "Go find the money, go find the site," was the message according to Harrington. "Convince the citizenry we need it and we can afford it." The city however did not provide money to the private fundraising campaign. It was ground swell grass roots support that eventually provided broad community participation.

While private sector leadership was crucial to the Portland campaign, the city did its important part to jump-start the

Left: Lobby, RiverCenter for the Performing Arts
Top right: Bill Heard Theatre, RiverCenter for the Performing Arts
Right: Studio Theater, RiverCenter for the Performing Arts

process by securing a key donor at the beginning. The ultimate success came though from a diverse base of community donors who made the project possible.

Development of a performing arts center will usually require many years of campaigning before the first shovel of dirt is turned. While the mayor and city council did their part to move the Portland process forward, at times players changed in politics and levels of support varied. Inevitably it was then up to the private sector supporters to keep the project dreams alive and moving forward.

A Georgia Project in the 1990s

When you look at projects at the end of the last decade, public support was reaching beyond what local government could do. State-level involvement was being used to move projects forward, including the New Jersey Performing Arts Center project in Newark and many others.

As costs for the performing arts center project type continued to grow in the 1990s, local and state governments became increasingly involved to make financing possible for construction. A success story is the RiverCenter for the Performing Arts in Columbus, Georgia, which established its key project leadership early with local and state involvement.

The Columbus Symphony was originally founded in the 1860s when the river town was an important stop between communities to the north and the Florida coast. That orchestra's success through the 20th century and the development of the rapidly growing Schwob School of Music at Columbus State University established in the minds of area residents the need for a multi-venue performing arts complex.

The Columbus-based Bradley-Turner Foundation provided funding and office support for a project manager to organize a performing arts center planning project involving both public and private partners. Rozier Dedwylder, a respected architect with strong community connections took the position. Established as the senior staff project champion, Dedwylder developed the project leadership, coordinating the detailed work of a range of specialists while anticipating

the requirements of outside stakeholders. The leadership in Columbus recognized that no one can do it alone; all successful project champions have the support of a strong and influential project team. RiverCenter's project team included a strategic mix of government staff and community advisors.

A key state legislator was selected to chair the RiverCenter project team. Its membership included the local university president, the mayor, the administrator of the community fundraising campaign, the chairperson of the city arts alliance and the project director himself. "The team's work must be task driven to get the center built," said Dedwylder at the time, "but its authority officially dissolved on opening night, leaving future management to the operating company created to operate the center."

State and local governments now recognize the advantages of shared service delivery with public-private partnerships including: project design, construction and procurement, financing,

operations and management, maintenance, marketing of services and communications. All such responsibilities fall under project management and are best handled with a strategically planned project team such as the one in Columbus.

"The days of the city leaders saying let's just build it in entirety with bond money are past us now" according to Dedwylder. The need for new partnership approaches becomes the rule rather than the exception. Projects are city driven, sometimes by the state, but all contain a private partnership effort.

The three-theater complex in Columbus is now owned by the Georgia Department of Natural Resources and the city deeded over the property to that state agency at the start of construction. Planning and project management was conducted by the Georgia State Financing and Investment

Above: Bill Heard Theatre, RiverCenter for the Performing Arts

Commission. Initial ownership and operational agreements included the Downtown Development Authority of Columbus, the Georgia Attorney General's Office, and the Board of Regents of the State University System. In addition, contract agreements included its operating company named RiverCenter, Inc., and the Community Project Foundation, created for private project fundraising. There were many players in the project and that is a consistent new trend with this building type.

It is important to note that a "secondary city" such as Columbus, with fewer than 300,000 residents, may do quite well in fundraising with leadership in local community gifts. In fact larger cities at times find it to be more difficult, as competition for philanthropic dollars may be quite intense.

Even in a city the size of Columbus the project faced early opposition from existing arts groups with their own capital needs. The answer there was a broad-based community campaign for RiverCenter that attracted over US$50 million in private funds, which ultimately benefited many local arts groups. A dozen different cultural organizations were significantly impacted by the effort. The Community Project Foundation leadership that ran the campaign eventually reorganized itself into a successful community foundation.

"The success with the RiverCenter in attracting significant involvement from the state government at US$25 million is attributed to Columbus' local elected leadership of representatives and senators, each of which spoke with a single voice in support of the project," noted Dedwylder.

A Texas Project for the New Century

Collin County is adjacent to the north border of Dallas in Texas. As one of America's fastest-growing counties and the most affluent of all in Texas, the need for its own cultural district was envisioned by the mayors of three of the county's key cities.

City capital improvement bonds were passed by Frisco, Plano and Allen for the project, which was defined as a Phase One plan to include a 2,100-seat multipurpose hall with outdoor performance and sculpture garden areas. More than 100 acres were donated by a local landowner with expectations that

additional adjacent property would create a unique arts park with a retail, office, and cultural mix. Future phases were targeted to provide for additional smaller theaters, a visual arts center, an education building, and a major amphitheater.

Each of the three owner cities committed US$19 million plus an annual commitment to support maintenance and operations. Added to the public support line, the Collin County government committed US$3 million to open space enhancements for the park including connecting trail systems and US$2.7 million for extension of a new road through the site.

From the beginning, emphasis was placed by local leaders on creating a home performance center for the Plano Symphony, Collin County Ballet, Cross Timbers Youth Orchestra, and other local groups. These groups, while successful, were frequently performing in venues to the south in Dallas County, as there were no sizeable facilities close to home.

To address the need for the new cultural complex, two new local corporations were created. The first, Arts of Collin County Foundation, was charged as a non-profit public charity to attract corporate and private donors. The second, Arts of Collin County Commission, was established as a local government corporation to hold ownership of the new facilities as well as serve the owner's role in design and construction.

Henry Lessner, President of the Arts of Collin County Foundation, clarified that "the strengths of the public-private collaboration effort is the key—three cities will accomplish something that none could do on their own." Rounding out the partnership with private dollars raised from a community fundraising campaign thus further linked the communities to support a major project for the greater good. Importantly, it was understood by all that the project is one larger than any of its constituent cities could undertake alone.

Visionary community leaders recognize that everyone has something to gain. The debate stimulates more awareness, as the press covers projects with recognized names associated with them. However even with such exposure, the public today does not read local papers and watch local television to the extent that they did in the past. Lessner pointed out that long-term residents are educated to the project on a day-by-day basis. "In the end it's all about word of mouth, one neighbor talking to the next, that communicates the project and its fundraising needs," he said.

People ultimately get involved for multiple reasons, convenience being a prime one. With the freeway by the new performing arts center, it is no more than 15 minutes away for most Collin County residents, compared to the long transit time to downtown Dallas and Fort Worth venues. That is a key link that sells having a project close by, whether the specific interest is in the local symphony, a touring Broadway show, or even a high school jazz concert in the park.

The attraction is to have a place where community comes together. More than just going to a show, having a project designed to allow for conversation and gatherings is important to many new performing arts centers. The Collin County design includes an indoor café as well as an outdoor grill, plus a martini bar with indoor and outdoor seating on a third-level sculpture terrace. Having these functions open on a daily basis along with an art gallery, gift shop, and indoor ticketing components enables the performing arts center to excel as a community destination.

"It's a big shift with performing arts venues to have their facilities used not just at show time but throughout the entire day. Making a destination place to go and have coffee and conversation makes it a true living room for the county," according to Lessner. This trend can be seen even with established institutions undergoing expansions for the entrance terrace areas at the Woodruff Center in Atlanta and Lincoln Center in New York.

The Collin County leadership recognized that capital campaign planning must happen from the outset. The public money committed is supplemented by private donors that catch the vision. Involvement from the early stages eventually translates into ownership that results in developing annual fund programs, endowment programs and significant numbers of season ticket holders.

Partnership Projects in Summary

New partnership strategies are evolving to make projects possible as the performing arts center building type becomes more costly. Higher costs for building materials, for labor, and for more and diverse technologies have continued to grow construction costs. The result is that partnerships between the public sector and private organizations for the financing, design, construction, ongoing maintenance, and creation of programming for performing arts centers are altogether more common.

Like the private business sector, government is increasingly working in a cooperative universe of activities. Governments at the local and state levels are looking for innovative solutions that involve collaborations both with other jurisdictions and the private and non-profit sectors.

Clearly, there are a variety of roles for both the public and private to be debated at all levels, from concept through opening night. The challenge is to determine the optimum mixture of public and private resources that will lead to the best methods of providing public services at acceptable levels of quality and cost.

The important message to the public is that there is much to gain by unique partnerships. Mutually beneficial agreements to suit all parties involved must be established and the advantages of the relationships has to be successfully communicated. Success comes through give and take, willingness to make concessions is important for all involved parties; it is the message of that success which must be sold to the public.

Both the public and the private sectors in today's economy are faced with many competing demands and limited resources. The public sector in particular now focuses on opportunities that use alternative means of delivering services including delegation to non-government partners and creating public–private arrangements. Small towns as well as major cities are forging partnerships in a variety of areas, from swimming pool and library construction projects with area school districts to fire training centers with neighboring municipalities.

Partnerships for new performing arts centers made possible by the private sector with support of local and state governments create interesting opportunities for everyone involved.

A good plan includes the development of clear lines of responsibilities (for example, council, staff, partners and stakeholders). The plan should eventually provide clear specifications and measurable performance outputs for the intended project in order to effectively monitor performance and minimize disputes.

In general, partnerships flourish because key leaders have exercised due diligence in planning, have established and engaged in a fair, open, and transparent process and have respected contractual obligations and performance requirements. Good governance implies all of the above.

For a performing arts center project to move beyond the idea stage it must secure leaders from the private sector. These leaders need to provide substantial donations themselves and have the capacity to attract other major donors. Once a private donor program is underway the public sector can then become fully engaged. For a project to be successful, public sector officials must work effectively with community leaders to sell the vision and ultimately bring the new performance center to reality.

Above: RiverCenter for the Performing Arts

147

All images: Models, New World Symphony

Above: Raoul-Jobin Theater, Palais Montcalm
Top right: Palais Montcalm
Right: Violon Du Roy, Raoul-Jobin Theater, Palais Montcalm

Anthony Sargent

151

with Keith Gerchak

The key first step of this project, which started in the second half of the 1980s, was to get two musical presenting organizations connected with it: the orchestra Northern Sinfonia and the folk and world traditional music development agency Folkworks. These two music presenters agreed and with the town of Gateshead and the regional arts funding body they formed a four-way partnership. That meant, right from the word go, it had in its planning the awareness of what an orchestra would need, what a mixed-genre music presenter would need, as well as what would be needed for education, because half of the building and half of the work that The Sage Gateshead does is education.

Musician and educator engagement came first. Initially, it was an organic, intuitive process; they were asked for a list of requirements each would have in this kind of center. Needs were played back by the design team in the form of design options. There were visits to chosen venues in Europe and North America. Some represented facilities that might in some respect be imitated, and others that generated problematic results, which The Sage Gateshead would be well advised to avoid. For five or six years a continuous two-way dialogue took place among the musicians and the design team, gaining over time a more precise sense of what the building would be like, how it would work, and what facilities it would need.

Then, there was research done to invite actual audiences to comment on the shape of the program that was emerging, to engage in a theoretical way with what the program might be like on paper. We engaged a leading UK-based market analysis

Left: Hall Two, The Sage Gateshead

team to test not just the contents of our program plans but also our proposed (primary and secondary) pricing structures and several other parameters. From all that data, achieved from a combination of face-to-face interviews and surveys, they then derived the size and makeup of our "theoretically accessible market," which then formed the basis of all our subsequent business planning. We then repeated what the Centre Pompidou did in Paris in the years running up to its 1977 opening. We created a very intensive, three-year pre-opening performance program, presenting in other venues work of a kind that was going to happen at The Sage Gateshead, before the building itself was finished. This allowed us to quickly move on from the theoretical confrontation with audiences to a more real world survey process, built around the events we were actually doing, which showed people simulations of the sort of programs forthcoming. From this we received precise audience information, and I must say it proved surprisingly reliable.

Very early on, we decided to make both the architect and the acoustician direct reports to the client. If you make the acoustician the secondary report below the architect, the obvious risk is that when you reach the inevitable moments of budgetary pressure with value engineering, the client may not get to hear about the acoustic compromises being made in that process, with potentially catastrophic results. Of all the facets of the performing arts facility that are difficult and expensive to improve once the hall has opened, the wrong acoustics are right at the top of the list. If the lighting is not right or the floor finishes are not right, you are talking in British terms of a few tens or hundreds of thousands of pounds; if the acoustics are wrong, you are probably talking in single or double figure millions.

There seemed to be a high degree of recognition of what the client's priorities were. That, I sensed, saved a lot of time—and therefore money—going down blind alleys. There was a primary focus on acoustic perfection in every space in the building—not just the three performing spaces, but also the 28 spaces used for teaching, rehearsing, recording, and other activities. At the start it was made clear that acoustic excellence in the performance, rehearsal, and learning spaces was paramount, followed by sound systems, light, and staging versatility, so that all the spaces could be used in many different ways.

For Foster and Partners Architects, there were particular things that were dear to their hearts; in professional terms, results that they wanted to achieve. There were particular bits of detailing about which Arup Acoustics felt very strongly. There were particular facilities that Theatre Projects Consultants wanted to be sure the building could offer. During the construction phase things come up in the real world, but Gateshead Council, who commissioned the building, was running—in British public sector terms—a very tight ship. So once the cost envelope had been agreed, if things then ran over along the way, other corresponding economies had to be found to balance out, and that was an organic process. It produced some difficult choices and some expressions of regret, but I think there was a very mature sense of partnership. Exactly the kind that I would expect to encounter in good artistic collaborations—where, in an unselfish way and very much looking at the quality of the finished whole, individual design partners were prepared to sacrifice particular things that they desired in order that the balance should emerge rightly.

There were two independent and freestanding musical organizations that were engaged in the initial planning of the process: Northern Sinfonia and Folkworks. At the point that the building was going to be built, a management company was being put together to run it. The first expectation was the normal European and North American model: that the (resident) orchestra would continue to be separate, that Folkworks would continue to be separate, and that there would be a third management of the hall itself, with potentially a fourth management of education. However, the more we looked at the dynamics of that traditional model, the more interested we became in finding ways of reducing some of the tensions that such models often produces in practice.

After considering several options, we finally decided to create a single, integrated management team covering the entire enterprise (building, musicians, and the whole performing and learning program) into which we absorbed both Northern Sinfonia and Folkworks. They ceased to exist as legally separate companies and staffs. Thus we do not now have a resident

Right: Foyer, The Sage Gateshead

orchestra; we operate more like an opera house, where we employ the orchestra as part of the total operation of the company, so Northern Sinfonia is referred to not as our resident orchestra, but as the orchestra of The Sage Gateshead. The orchestra records and broadcasts as well as gives concerts and undertakes education work, and those activities are now all run by the same company. We are also responsible for programming all the music performances in the building, something in the vicinity of 450 a year, with a much lower proportion than usual of pure rentals in order to maximize our quality control over the whole program. We offer community and education programming (we refer to it as Learning and Participation), dealing with roughly half a million consumers a year across all 10,000 square miles of the north of England in all kinds of music,

as well as three national contracts, making ours (in terms of kinds of music, the range of ability levels we accept, geography, and demography) the most extensive music learning program in the world run by a single institution. And, we run the building physically. So some things, which in a normal hall would be external collaborations with other companies, here are internal functions of the different departments and teams of people working within one company.

It is an unusual challenge in building this sort of project to start by amalgamating three groups of people, and when it does happen the motive is often a resource issue—to achieve some rationalization of a budget through sharing infrastructure resources, which makes perfectly good business sense. However that was not the motive here, although we did indeed achieve that. The motive was to bring the two principal artistic collaborating bodies into the core of the main management of the whole company. Its success was not a foregone conclusion. It involved asking organizations—one of them 40 years old, the other 20 years old—to surrender all their independence, to surrender particularly the comfort of having direct subsidy from regional and central government, and instead to be part of a single, large-scale company with all the associated loss of sovereignty, loss of control, and inevitably some loss of speed of response and decision-taking. We started with 38 employees, and we now have an employment footprint of well over 500, so obviously the fleetness of foot that you can achieve managerially with 38 employees, and the management structures you need, are quite different.

It was a process that took 18 months to execute, and it also took an enormous amount of political care, particularly in avoiding any language that gave any impression of a takeover. The noun we consistently used was integration, to try to give a sense that these were sovereign bodies merging their interests. What I have probably made sound very easy and rather automatic was actually a very careful and sensitive process, which had enormous capacity to go wrong and subsequently derail the whole journey. We have created a management metaphor for everybody working here—to treat the building and the relationship with its users and audiences in exactly the way they would treat visitors in our own homes. It has produced an unusually personal kind of service for an industrial-scale facility.

I am very proud of our culture and texture; it did not establish itself. It is at every level of encounter, whether it is the voice you hear when you call to book a ticket, or the people who show you to your seat, or the people that teach you if you come as a student, or indeed our performing musicians. I wanted very much to create an illusion that people were visiting a small neighborhood facility, where they knew all the people on first name terms, and if they did not have the money at the bar, it was taken on trust that they would come back the next day and pay—the sort of easy informalities that are the norm in very small communities. I attribute this unified experience,

the coherent tone of voice expressed through both architecture and staff, as a direct consequence of an awareness from the start that the building would be run by a completely integrated management.

Physically, The Sage Gateshead is also designed as a supremely integrated building. The music education center is not in a separate facility. You do not go through a back door to reach it, and you can hear the sound of people milling about and chatting in the education area foyer pretty much wherever you are in the building's public spaces. The three performance halls open onto a single concourse (which also contains our four bars, café, and brasserie) so when, as often, we have concerts in more than one hall on the same night, people that may know each other—because we are not a big community here—may meet, and that is a very attractive circumstance.

We have just two doors for the public (one at each end of the building's concourse), which are used regardless of whether you are a corporate client coming for a conference, an 8-year-old coming for a piano lesson, an audience member, or just a casual visitor. In that sense it is an immensely democratic building. I think people's natural instinct, the minute they cross the threshold, is to feel some element of welcome directly from the architecture.

The Sage Gateshead is all about being friendly and informal, easy to use and to navigate, and comfortable to sit in. Perhaps some of the building's almost spiritual qualities were communicated to the design team unconsciously. It may simply be that they are a reflection of the initial 38 people working here. To welcome visitors and offer them an agreeable and relaxing experience were not particular conditions we outlined: we briefed for effectiveness and cost efficiency and all of those obvious things. Whether subliminal or otherwise, the design team intuited these human, ethereal qualities, and as a result, we have a building that itself goes the extra mile in being pleasant and receptive to all who visit.

Left: Hall One, The Sage Gateshead
Following pages: The Sage Gateshead

155

Left: Moores Opera House, Moores School of Music, University of Houston

Top: Moores School of Music, University of Houston

Above: Lobby ceiling art by Frank Stella, Moores School of Music, University of Houston

Left and above: Moores Opera House, Moores School of Music, University of Houston

Susan Hilferty

163

with Keith Gerchak

My life in the theater started in high school where, in addition to classes, I was busy drawing, making my own clothes, and acting in plays. At Syracuse University, as a painting major with a minor in fashion design, I started working backstage and seeing theater, and I began to understand what designing for the theater was.

In my junior year in London, I saw more than 40 shows, including the original productions of *The Rocky Horror Show*, *Equus*, and Athol Fugard's *Sizwe Banzi is Dead*. It was then that I began to understand that theater design is simple storytelling—that everything and everyone must serve the text and that we all must find our roles within this world. To make great theater, you need a great stage manager, you need a great actor, you need a great dressmaker, a great wardrobe person, as well as a great designer and a great director.

There comes a moment when a developing designer needs to find a way to focus on their process. After working in New York City for several years, designing productions and working in costume shops, I went to the Yale School of Drama for an MFA in Theatre Design. My years in graduate school allowed me to develop myself as an artist. Theater is a collaborative art form, and it is hard to say "OK, I am just going to go into my studio for three years and figure it out." You have to be in a place that allows you to be connected to other artists and artisans, but not be controlled by them— where you can watch how directors are developing themselves, as well as the actors, writers, and other designers.

Left: Stanley Williams Studio, School of American Ballet

Left: Studio 6, Upper Level, School of American Ballet
Above: Stanley Williams Studio, School of American Ballet

I believe a good program divides the training carefully between production and studio work, and not all are good programs. In many, student designers are brought in just for production, and never have the contemplative moments—the "dream time" that happens in a studio, which is necessary to develop a process of designing. Every artist has to have time to expand their own experience of the universe. They have to read, travel, and listen. What do you bring to the table if you have not had experiences outside of the theater? A designer has to step outside herself and travel into the future, to China, or to Queens. She must speak the language of Shakespeare and Bollywood. Each text demands that we work in a new world.

Many worlds make up professional theater. There is the world of downtown showcases, the world of not-for-profit theater, and the world of commercial theater. I hope that the program at New York University's Tisch School of The Arts will reflect as much as possible the not-for-profit model of the regional and resident theaters around the country: the Goodman in Chicago, ACT in San Francisco, the Guthrie in Minneapolis, or Second Stage here in New York. These resident theater companies are usually connected to a building and a community. They are bigger than the organization. When I say I am part of the La Jolla Playhouse, it means I am part of La Jolla, a part of its history, part of the team inside the building and in the community. Those relationships have been developing since those theaters began, and without them, those companies would fade away.

The relationships in commercial theater are very different. When you begin a Broadway musical, you do not necessarily know what theater you are going to go into. You know that you are going to be on "Broadway"—that mythical dream, which is really only a district defined by boundaries and the number of seats in the house. You have to work harder to do a commercial production, because you create from scratch the whole infrastructure that already exists in the not-for-profit theater. You have to bring in your producer, your company manager, and your stage manager. It is much different when you do not have a home. You must create these connections.

In commercial theater, everybody is trying to figure out where they are within the newly formed hierarchy. For instance, years ago on a commercial production, you would get a costume designer, a lighting designer, and a set designer, who would each go to one independent specialty shop that would then build a whole show. Now, the scenery is often painted in one shop and the turntables built in another; it has become so splintered. The fracturing of the elements requires there to be a liaison between the production team and the producers. So they introduced the role of a Production Supervisor, which is now in every Broadway show. The Production Supervisor is responsible for the technical part of a production. They deal with lights, they deal with props, they deal with sound—they deal with everything, except they rarely deal with the clothes. When I did *Wicked*, we went to 21 shops. Just organizing 21 shops is a full-time job, and today that responsibility falls on the costume designer and her associate.

At NYU, we are hard at work on creating the best environment we can for making and teaching theater. Our building project for the Tisch Institute of the Performing Arts will dramatically increase the quantity and quality of spaces for instruction and performance for both undergraduate and graduate programs in dance, drama, production design, and graduate musical theater writing. The first step has been to define our beliefs. We have identified what it is that our individual departments currently do and dreamt of what we want to do in the future. It is an important step, because like any design, changing it once it is built is much more complicated than dreaming about it.

It has been a tough, rewarding process. It has required us to establish clearly the way that we want to collaborate. Collaborating does not mean everybody is having a good time together; it means communicating. Collaborating is difficult because you have to give things up. You are constantly negotiating. To do it well, you have to keep identifying your values and together say "us" instead of "me," knowing that there are certain things that are essential for each department and certain common threads.

The next thing we did is visit theaters. It is like bringing sketches or a model into a conversation; this has allowed us the opportunity to see full-size solutions to the problem of defining what a theater can be. It has been very clear in all the institutions we visited that the physical structures reflect their mission. To go into a theater and to see, quite literally, how the structure connects to the hearts of those companies has helped us to define our own needs.

The building design process is no different than the designing of a show. You read the text, wrestle with it, try to understand it, look for inspiration, and then start to put it into two and three dimensions. Then you evaluate and re-evaluate. Does your idea work? Does it do what you set out to do?

The next phase is more concrete. In the first phase, the dream phase, you know that you are going to design something that is bigger than anything that is accomplishable. But after that dream phase, you now know the story and everything so well that you can cut the non-essentials. You can start to make changes and believe that you are not going to lose the core value of the whole.

From the very first production meeting of a show, the whole team is trying to develop the rules of that particular production—its own vocabulary, its own language. Even if

I am working with the same team on another production, we must create different worlds for different shows. In the rehearsal room, we have the freedom to develop this common language. It can be terrifying for a designer, because the design has to be concretized at some early point, but we must stay open to new developments.

It is the same when we are working on our new building. We have established a basic vocabulary, and we examine every choice to see if it can better fulfill our program. Can we embody our values if we move the dressing rooms to another floor? Do we shortchange the education of our students in theaters that fail to allow entrances onto the stage from every side, including from above and below? These are only two of a million questions that must be asked.

It is wildly interesting to be involved in the idea of building from scratch an environment for teaching theater at NYU. We have to be quite clear about who we are and what we need. It has been the largest production of many of our lives, and like any show, there is the possibility of rave reviews or scathing ones. But, I am not worried about the immediate outcome. I believe that we will build a program that will serve who we are today. It will be interesting to see if we have allowed ourselves enough room to grow in the coming years. Let us talk again in 20 years.

Right: Lounge between Studio 6 and Studio 7, School of American Ballet

Above, bottom right, top far right: Roundhouse
Top right: Historic exterior circa 1940

Left: 6,000-Seat Performance Hall, Crocus International – Expo 3
Top and above: Lobby, Crocus International – Expo 3

Ed Herendeen

173

The time has come to build a new home for the Contemporary American Theater Festival. Since 1991 the Theater Festival, a non-profit professional theater dedicated to producing and developing new American theater, had been operating independently under a special agreement with our host Shepherd University. Over the years the Theater Festival has developed a solid national reputation as a home for new American plays. As a result of our ten-year strategic plan we determined that it was necessary to build a new facility that would secure our position as an innovative theater company and producer of new American literature for stage.

Shepherd University also had plans to build a new facility for its outstanding Visual Arts program. This created an opportunity for the Theater Festival and the University to begin a dialogue, which resulted in an extraordinary alliance between a liberal arts institution, a newly created School of Contemporary Art and Theater, and a professional theater. In an era of innovation, it is imperative that arts organizations and universities have a well-defined purpose. Having a purpose justifies the risks associated with innovation. Purpose drives strategy and it helps shape the choices we make.

The partnership between the Contemporary American Theater Festival and Shepherd University is another step in the recognition that colleges and universities are more than patrons of the arts; they are creative institutions peopled by individuals who are excited by the opportunity to benefit from

Left: Center for Contemporary Arts, Shepherd University

one of our oldest art forms. We recognize that this unique and special partnership is a significant development not just in the life of this fine university, but also in the life of our community, region, and nation.

To achieve our combined goals we created a joint partnership with the Board of Trustees of the Contemporary American Theater Festival, the Shepherd University Board of Governors, and the School of Contemporary Art and Theater to build a new center for contemporary art. We would create a world-class facility for the purpose of developing, producing and presenting bold new works of art as well as mentoring and educating a new generation of emerging contemporary artists and conceptual thinkers.

Together the University's Board of Governors, its Foundation, and its Alumni Board joined with CATF's Board of Trustees to secure funding from the state, individual donors, and foundations. This was the first time that these four boards had worked together toward a common goal. A 50-year Memorandum of Understanding was developed between CATF and Shepherd University whereby the University would own and maintain the Arts Center and CATF would be granted use of the facilities rent free. The agreement between the University and CATF is renewable.

United by our collective purpose we began a revolutionary conversation. Starting with a blank canvas, and unleashed from the traditions and expectations of the culture of academia, we created a partnership where we could freely envision a new center for contemporary art. Our newly created alliance imagined a collaborative environment where the boundaries between a professional theater and academic programs in visual art and theater would be blurred, and where the function between disciplines would become sources of energy and inspiration. We believed that it was possible to invent a new culture within a university setting, where we could make art in a shared, even ideal, atmosphere— a revolutionary undertaking based on the creative process.

Every aspect of our new facility, from its location, to the choice of architects, to the choice of design, to its function was discussed in concert with an emerging vision of creating

an ideal environment for making art. We were committed to creating an atmosphere of risk-taking conducive to bold, daring work. This was a win–win relationship for all of us.

Among others, our building committee included the Chair of the Department of Contemporary Art and Theater and the Dean of the School of Arts and Humanities. Collectively we began talking and playing around with new ideas, new forms, and new ways of working together that are vital to innovative thinking. This became the heart of our new alliance. We envisioned a workplace that would inspire and engage artists, students, and the community.

Our joint venture began with an idea. And our ultimate success depended upon innovation and a continuing, constant flow of imagination and collaboration. We were determined to break the bonds of a traditional academic–bureaucratic structure with its need for predictability and conformance to accepted norms. We formed a transparent partnership united by a single purpose—creating new works of art and mentoring the next generation of contemporary artists.

We agreed to share budgets, space, and our collective thinking. The sculpture/welding studio and the scene/prop shop would share an inspiring warehouse space. Rehearsal spaces would double as art studios for performance art exhibits, performances, and critiques.

Our committee traveled together with our architects to see some of their other completed arts centers and develop a common frame of reference. We went a step further, inviting prominent American playwrights, Lee Blessing, Richard Dresser, Theresa Rebeck, Stephen Belber, and others to join us in a conversation at the office of Holzman Moss Architecture during our planning process. They shared their insights on the importance of creating theater spaces ideal for listening, seeing and experiencing "live storytelling." We discussed the value of "silence." Rebeck remarked, "When I walk into the new Center, I want to know that something 'important' happens here." Playwrights are the primary artists in theater and their comments were vital to our purpose and mission. It was an extraordinary conversation and measure of collaboration.

Top: Gallery, Center for Contemporary Arts, Shepherd University
Above: Center for Contemporary Arts, Shepherd University

We believe that it is possible to imagine creativity thriving in an academic bureaucracy, or even academia welcoming creative thought. At first we had no idea of either the challenges or full implications of our endeavor. But we gradually discovered that our unique partnership had the potential to change the way a professional theater and a school of Art and Theater did business.

Central to our new center will be an expanded festival of new American plays, visual and performance art exhibits, artistic and educational programs, and a community for professional artists, mentors, and master teachers. Through the exploration and creation of new American theater and visual art we will engage our community in conversation, debate, intellectual curiosity, and emotional connection.

The Center for Contemporary Art began in a think tank of ideas and colliding cultures. Everything was open for discussion and the atmosphere was intense, irreverent, sometimes abrasive but always joyous. We were building a new home for art and all the raw elements of a truly groundbreaking environment were in place. Our purpose was larger than we could have imagined and everyone: painters, sculptors, photographers, printmakers, graphic designers, scholars, playwrights, actors, directors, technicians, and administrative staff were stretched beyond their job descriptions. And we all recognized how our disciplines overlapped. This resulted in periods of inspired exhilaration. We were committed to the concept of collaboration, creative thinking, problem solving, and a process of intuitive trial and error. This enabled us to create an atmosphere that encouraged

risk taking and discovery. We formed a working alliance of thinkers dedicated to exploring new ways of nurturing and producing innovative work.

Through this process I learned to listen to our group and welcome different opinions. "Collective creativity" involves a large number of people from different disciplines working together to solve many problems. Creativity must be present at every level of the design and planning process. Innovation does not take place in isolation and need not be competitive. We created a culture around our shared goal and involved others to be part of it. All of us had an extraordinary amount of curiosity about our project; we were not afraid to challenge the status quo and we were not afraid to fail.

I further learned that the need to communicate vision and purpose for the project must extend to all those who in any way help shape its future. From experience, I now know the value of imbuing an atmosphere of creativity all the way through the construction process, and the challenge of motivating and inspiring contractors to embrace our commitment to excellence.

The role of creativity and our willingness to collaborate was the driving force in the success of our joint venture. Partnerships are relationships based on trust and the ability to listen. The formula for our successful enterprise was a combination of a sharp artistic focus, a smart and objective business plan, and a "big picture" strategic plan. We formed an artistic partnership with passion, blind faith, talent, naiveté, mutual purpose, and a desire to say something important. Ultimately we discovered that our partnership was about much more than bricks and mortar.

Left: Rehearsal space, Center for Contemporary Arts, Shepherd University

Top right: Painting studio, Center for Contemporary Arts, Shepherd University

Right: Copper cladding, Center for Contemporary Arts, Shepherd University

The Eli and Edythe Broad Stage, Santa Monica College
Santa Monica, California, USA

Left and above: The Eli and Edythe Broad Stage, Santa Monica College

All images: The Eli and Edythe Broad Stage, Santa Monica College

Duncan Webb

183

Partnerships and collaborations are critically important to the development and operation of performing arts facilities, not just their planning and design. Over the past 20 years, I have written more than 250 feasibility studies and business for new and existing facilities. And as time passes, I have come to see that these projects are so complicated and expensive that they simply cannot get open and stay open without partners and partnerships.

So what makes a good partnership? It is one where two or more parties come together to achieve something that they cannot do on their own. They are able to clearly express their roles and expectations coming in. They have the financial and human resources necessary to make the commitment to stay involved for the duration. And they are good communicators, able to express concerns and resolve conflicts through all of the turmoil that is inevitable with these projects.

Here are some of my favorite developmental and operating partnerships and collaborations that we have been involved with over the years:

The Chandler Center for the Arts is a pioneering partnership, a 1,550-seat hall with two rotating pods that can divide one large hall into three smaller theaters. Built in 1988, the center is jointly owned and operated by the city of Chandler and Chandler Unified School District. Both entities contributed to the center's construction and support its ongoing operation.

Top left and left: Sun Valley Pavilion

A third arm, the Chandler Cultural Foundation, was established and then contracted by the city of Chandler to fundraise and present public programs at the center. The Foundation also continues to build an endowment to support the center's long-term sustainability.

At the very beginning of the venture, these three partners established a clear and concise joint use agreement that defines which groups have priority access to the halls during certain times, and then sets the cost and conditions of access. Twenty years later, that agreement is still in place with scheduling and access policies that allow school, city, and public programs to effectively share and successfully operate the facility as a true community resource, delivering quality and affordable arts programs to the community. In fact, the center is in use more than 300 days a year, is home to more than 40 groups from throughout the Phoenix metropolitan area, draws annual audiences of more than 280,000, and is known as one of the only venues in the Valley that provides quality programming at a highly competitive cost. As the only indoor cultural venue in Chandler, and with audiences that represent three-quarters of all local arts attendance, activity at the center instigates a large portion of the annual US$7.1 million economic impact of the arts in Chandler. And it is currently serving as an anchor for impressive downtown revitalization that includes a mix of residential, retail, and restaurant outlets as well as significant investment in façade and tenant improvements.

In 2000, Proctors Theater in Schenectady, New York was considering the need to replace the stagehouse on this historic 2,700-seat theater in order to accommodate larger touring musicals. But when it started working with Metroplex, a New York State development agency, it conceived of a plan to become the anchor of a downtown cultural district. By convincing the agency that the renovated and expanded theater would have significant economic impacts, Proctors was able to access state funding for its own work and then help direct additional funding to neighboring projects, including the renovation of an adjacent four-story building. Thus, the project expanded to include small performance and rehearsal space, banquet and meeting facilities, a partnership with the Schenectady County community college to offer classes and internships at the theater, the development of a large-format

film venue for school-children and, most interestingly, a new mechanical plant that sells hot and cold water to other enterprises along the block.

As a result of this partnership, there has been US$250 million in downtown development in Schenectady, with another US$150 million now in the planning stage. In addition, the downtown vacancy rate has dropped from 60 to 20 percent in the last four years. The new mechanical plant has reduced the theater's carbon footprint by 260 lbs/hour and is now serving three commercial neighbors. The GE Theater, which has a capacity of 400 people and can support both live performance and large-format film, has been particularly busy, often supporting three performances a day by local non-profit groups, schools and corporations.

In 2002, we helped the city of Durham, North Carolina assess the need for performing arts facilities for its community and the opportunity for downtown revitalization through the arts. This led to a plan for a large, new hall that might bring touring arts and entertainment to Durham. To develop and operate such new facilities, we helped the city solicit bids from the private sector, asking for a joint bid from developers, designers, and operators. The selected team was lead by local architect Szostak and Associates, with developers Garfield Traub and Clear Channel Entertainment as the operator. Clear Channel pulled out of the project in 2006, leading the city to issue a second RFP for operators. The group selected was Professional Facilities Management in partnership with the Nederlander Organization.

The challenge of the project was that the development team had to develop a financing plan to build and sustain the theater, given only a US$1.4-million annual commitment of local occupancy taxes for 28 years. After determining what might be financed through tax-free municipal bonds, the team then sought out corporate-sector partners to purchase naming rights. Duke University provided US$7.5 million in funding to guarantee access to the hall for the American Dance Festival, a major annual festival based at Duke these last 25 years. The total project budget was US$47 million, and the hall opened in late 2008.

The operating partnership is particularly important. Though the city is the owner of the land and building, capital improvements will be funded with a $1.50 per ticket surcharge. And all financial risk is with the operator, who is obliged to animate the building with a range of cultural and commercial programming through a five-year contract. In the first season it will host a four-show Broadway series and a number of one-night performances. The American Dance Festival will move into the building for its summer 2009 festival, programming the hall for four full weeks.

The project has already had a significant impact on downtown development in Durham. Projects underway are valued at US$270 million, with three different developers working on commercial and residential developments.

After several years as a nomadic but groundbreaking force in modern dance, the Bill T. Jones/Arnie Zane Dance Company wants to put down roots in the Harlem neighborhood of New York City. The decision is timely, as the 125th Street Business District, historically serving as the neighborhood's energetic center, is going through an impressive revitalization. The project began in 2005 when the company approached the New York City Department of Economic Development about the possibility of finding HUD (the federal department of Housing and Urban Development) properties available for redevelopment. Though no such properties were available, the city offered the dance company an opportunity to join a private developer seeking a community partner for a new mixed-use development along 125th Street, which then led to commitments of funding from HUD, the city's Economic Development Office, the Borough President's Office and the Upper Manhattan Empowerment Zone. In addition, the project has qualified for New Market Tax Credits, which will support a level of debt financing for the facility. The developer is now facing significant challenges in securing financing for the larger project and in attracting retail tenants to the mixed-use development, so the company is expanding its search for alternative sites along the 125th Street corridor. They have just completed a fundraising feasibility study to set a private-sector goal for the capital campaign and will begin fundraising shortly.

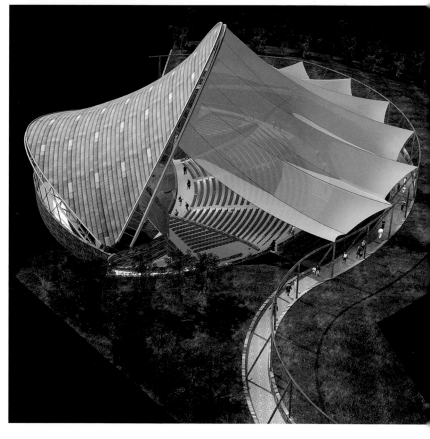

Top: Sun Valley Pavilion
Bottom: Rendering, Sun Valley Pavilion

This project reflects many of the current challenges in facility development collaborations. It had already gone through a series of twists and turns with the fluctuating economy, changes in political priorities and volatility in the local real estate market. It has been very difficult and complicated to hold together partners from the public sector, private sector, and the nonprofit sector. And each element of the funding plan comes with covenants and conditions that might tie the company and project into knots. But all of this will be worth it if the project is completed. The community will benefit from quality, affordable, and relevant programs, the developer will receive both monetary and public relations credit for playing a hand in developing the Company's home, the city will benefit from the company's presence and resulting foot traffic, and the company will further solidify its identity and future by expanding programs in a permanent location.

In April 2007, our firm hosted a think-tank in New York City entitled "The Performing Arts Center of 2032". We invited performing arts facility managers from around North America to spend two days with us thinking about the future of audiences, the disciplines, arts funding, and the buildings themselves. Through these discussions, it became clear that partnerships and collaborations are likely to become even more important as we look to the future. Specifically:

We are starting to see colleges and universities pursue the development of cultural facilities outside of a traditional

campus environment. This opens up a whole new world of opportunities, as educational institutions can become a catalytic force in downtown revitalization and the adaptive re-use of existing structures.

The arts palace is giving way to the arts district, which is allowing communities to partner with commercial developers to pursue projects with multiple facilities that drive commercial development and create cultural destinations.

The growth sector in the performing arts is in the area of active participation, where people of all ages wish to sing, act, and dance themselves. Colleges and universities are thus becoming effective partners in buildings with classrooms, rehearsal halls, and appropriate performance spaces, supporting the needs of the amateur and avocational artist.

Arts education programs in performing arts facilities have advanced tremendously in recent years through partnerships between facilities and school districts. Not long ago, it was all about busing schoolkids in for a matinee performance of a touring show. Today, many larger facilities have more than a dozen different education programs, including camps, residencies, master classes, competitions, teacher training, and curriculum development. And we expect further growth in this area as more performing arts facilities find funding sources supportive of these partnerships.

Performing arts facilities have become increasingly active as producers and investors in the work they present, most notably with the Independent Producers Network, an association whose members are given the opportunity to invest in Broadway productions and thus gain earlier access to the national tour of that show. We expect that same model to be replicated in other disciplines, as facilities and artists partner on the commissioning and development of work suitable for touring.

Left and above: Sun Valley Pavilion

Left: Allen Theater, Student Union Building, Texas Tech University
Above: Student Union Building, Texas Tech University

190

Above: Student Union Building, Texas Tech University
Right: 100-seat Escondito Theater, Student Union Building, Texas Tech University

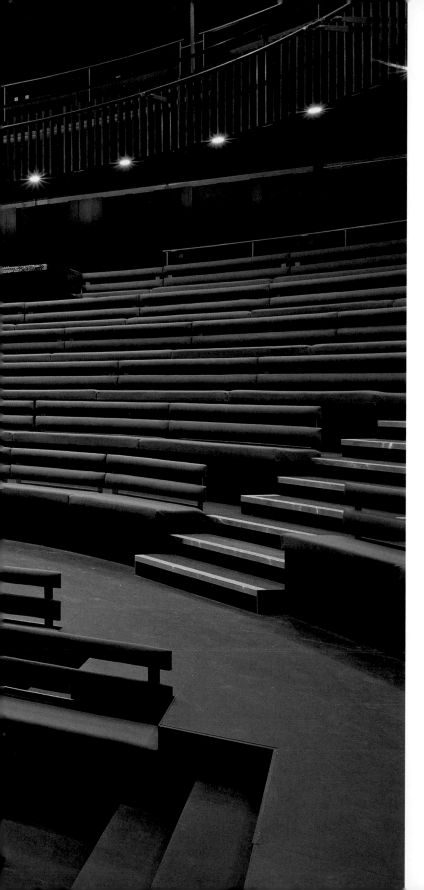

Richard Dresser

193

As the most collaborative of arts, theater by its very nature engenders partnerships. The best creative experiences of my life have come out of intense collaborations with directors and actors working together on a shared vision of what a particular play can be.

Another, more rare kind of partnership, between a playwright and a theater, can be of enormous value to both parties. A play does not truly exist until it is performed in front of an audience, so playwrights have a difficult time progressing in their craft until they are able to consistently see their work on stage. Readings and workshops can be of great value in the development of a script, but there is simply no substitute for a fully realized production where the strengths and weaknesses of a play are (sometimes painfully) revealed. When a theater makes a commitment to a playwright, he or she has the enormous advantage of seeing one play after another fully mounted, and the theater gets to intimately participate in a writer's artistic evolution.

My partnership with the Contemporary American Theater Festival (CATF) did not get off to an auspicious beginning, as I was not present for it. I was living in Los Angeles when I got a call from a playwright friend who told me that he had just attended an extraordinary production of my play *Below the Belt*, and I should make every effort to see it. I asked where it was being staged and when he said, "West Virginia," I quickly decided that my schedule was a bit too tight to allow for such a trip. I soon discovered how misguided my dismissal of this

Left: Weston Theatre, Unicorn Children's Centre

fledgling theater in Shepherdstown, West Virginia really was. I met with Ed Herendeen, the founder and Artistic Director, and he said he would like to do another of my plays if I would show up for it. It did not seem to be an unreasonable demand. I arrived the next summer for the season-opening barbecue, heard Ed's hugely ambitious vision for the theater, took a good look at the immensely gifted collection of actors and designers ready to devote the coming months to launching four new American plays, and was hooked.

It has been a truly dynamic partnership with CATF that has carried through seven of my plays. While I have worked with different directors, actors, and designers on these plays, the commitment from the theater has been absolutely constant. When the shared goal of both parties is to put the strongest work possible on stage, disagreements are productive and problems have a way of getting solved. For me, one of the hallmarks of a productive partnership is that nothing is taken for granted. I do not assume CATF will produce my work any more than they assume I will bring them my next play. This keeps the partnership alive and not limited in any way by past assumptions.

One of the more intriguing aspects of my partnership with CATF concerns the new theaters, which are phase three of the Contemporary Arts Center. At that long-ago barbecue when

Ed described his vision for a new building with theaters, rehearsal halls, and offices, I frankly dismissed it as a fantasy. But he persevered, and that of course is what artists do— make their dreams real. At various points through the years, Ed consulted with playwrights about what we most wanted in a theater, giving us the opportunity to look at plans and models and talk directly to the architects about acoustics, intimacy with the audience, and flexible stages to accommodate the widest variety of plays. It is truly rare that playwrights are involved in the most basic aspect of a theatrical experience, the physical structure in which our plays are staged. Clearly, where a play is staged has a profound effect on how it is received by the audience. A two-character play might be heartbreaking when presented in an intimate space but be lost and lifeless on a cavernous proscenium stage.

Playwrights lead a freelance life. There are occasional grants and commissions, but for the most part one is alone in a room creating a play, then trying to find a home where the play will be respected, nurtured, and realized as fully as possible. While there are no guarantees that my work will be produced at CATF— and there should not be—knowing that I have such a dynamic ongoing partnership with a thriving theater is a huge incentive to write the next play. Which is all any playwright could ask.

Left: Foyer, Unicorn Children's Centre
Right: Unicorn Children's Centre

Top left, above, right: Performing Arts Center, Texas A&M University-Corpus Christi
Left: Lobby, Performing Arts Center, Texas A&M University-Corpus Christi

Above: Opera students, Performing Arts Center, Texas A&M University-Corpus Christi
Right: Entrance, Performing Arts Center, Texas A&M University-Corpus Christi

Howard Shalwitz

Looking back, I have a favorite moment in the long design process that led to the creation of Woolly Mammoth's new theater. It was during an exhausting meeting with our entire team, including our architects, theater design consultants, acoustician, construction engineer, mechanical, electrical and plumbing consultant, Woolly's technical director and myself. The topic was mundane but critical: how to get air flowing quietly and efficiently through the space. Ideas were batted around, sketches were created and discarded. There was heated debate about everyone's needs, which were often at odds with one another.

At a certain point it struck me—this is precisely what we go through when we design the set, costumes, lighting, and sound for a play. The director and various designers sit around a table, brainstorm, listen, make sketches, try to influence and inspire one another, and gradually work things out. People express amazement at this kind of collaboration in the theater, and the same is true about architecture. They look at a play, or a building, and try to imagine how the ideas came together. What would it be like, they wonder, to be part of such a complex creative undertaking? For my part, working with architects and theater designers for the first time, I felt a tremendous kinship.

The number of collaborators on our project was perhaps greater than usual, including the federal government, the city government, a private developer, a multilayered design team, generous private donors, and of course, Woolly Mammoth's dedicated Board, staff, and artists.

Far left and left: Woolly Mammoth Theatre

Founded in Washington, D.C. in 1980, Woolly Mammoth quickly emerged as one of the nation's leading "alternative" theaters. We never aspired to be a "regional" theater per se, but to carve out a more unique niche through an aggressive acting style, challenging plays, and an emphasis on new work. Located in a church for six seasons and a tiny warehouse for 13, we began searching for a more permanent home around 1993, hoping to purchase and convert a run-down building in one of our city's transitional neighborhoods. Then, in 1998, we heard about a competition for the development rights to Parcel 457-C, half a city block owned by the federal government in the heart of downtown.

The Request for Proposal called for mostly apartments and street-level retail, but also included a mandate for a small amount of arts space with a "preference" for a live theater. This farsighted plan stemmed from the Pennsylvania Avenue Development Corporation, a quasi-governmental agency created in the 1960s to oversee redevelopment of one of the nation's most famous avenues from the Capitol Building to the White House. However, the Agency's arts mandate was a stick with no carrot. They offered no incentives for the developer, relying simply on the competitive process to induce realistic deals between competing developers and potential arts users.

During the competition phase of the project, various private developers affiliated themselves with different theater organizations. Many developers expressed an interest in working with Woolly Mammoth—we had a good reputation, a sophisticated board, and reasonable space requirements. After meeting with many developers, we decided to make an exclusive deal with JPI of Texas, a developer who was fairly new to the D.C. market. We knew and admired their architect, Esocoff & Associates, and our research made us believe they would offer the most money for the property and therefore win the bid.

Our judgment was right. In 2000, the Agency awarded JPI the right to purchase and develop Parcel 457-C. Woolly Mammoth quickly formed a Building Committee and established three goals: (1) to build one of the great small theaters in the world; (2) to fully reflect Woolly's risk-taking mission and aesthetics; and (3) to make the project affordable for our community. (Achieving the second goal, we often said, would help us resolve the tension between the first and third.) We began an extensive search for an architect, reviewed submissions from 80 firms, interviewed six, and visited projects throughout the northeast designed by our finalists. We also met with three theater design consulting firms and toured their projects in New York, Toronto, and elsewhere.

During the competition, it had been determined that the theater would be located, for structural reasons, under the central courtyard of a 12-story apartment tower, necessitating a fairly long passage from the street to the theater. Our street entrance, framed by an historic façade, would be adjacent to a residential entry courtyard, and our overall footprint of 30,000 square feet would be arranged in a complex pattern on three floors. The architect we hired, McInturff Architects of Bethesda, Maryland, was able to help us understand the three-dimensional challenge of unifying this complex space. Mark McInturff's modernist aesthetic matched our own, and he had clear ideas about controlling costs—though he had never designed a theater before.

We paired McInturff's boutique-sized firm with one of the largest theater design consulting firms in the world, Theatre Projects Consultants. I was predisposed toward TPC because of my love for the Cottesloe and Tricycle Theatres in London. We felt the firm had the depth and flexibility to give our relatively small project the attention it deserved. As it turned out, the collaboration between McInturff and TPC was the foundation of our success.

If there is one piece of advice I would offer to other theaters embarking on construction projects, it's this: do not shortchange the search for your design team. There are a number of outstanding firms who will no doubt be interested; seeing their work and hearing their ideas will transform your vision.

Left and top right: Lobby, Woolly Mammoth Theatre
Right: Green Room, Woolly Mammoth Theatre

While I was pushing the selection process forward, Woolly's Managing Director dove into detailed negotiations with JPI, supported by our Board President and pro bono legal counsel. The negotiations ultimately lasted two and a half years. During the competition phase, Woolly tried to get JPI to commit to specific terms, but they would only agree to an exclusive negotiation period, which would begin after the project was awarded. At that point, JPI asked us to pay US$4 million for the raw space, but we insisted we could only raise enough money for the interior build out. We held our ground on this key point, counting on the fact that neither JPI nor the federal government would want to start over with another theater company. Ultimately, JPI agreed to a remarkably generous deal—Woolly would rent the raw shell for US$1 per year for 30 years, pay our share of common area maintenance costs, and handle our own interior construction. Subsequently, we had to kick in US$300,000 for some specialized construction costs accrued by the developer.

Throughout the design process, there was a productive give and take between our architect (McInturff) and the base building architect (Esocoff). Columns and walls were moved, ceilings raised, and parking slabs lowered. After our rough design was completed, JPI opted to add more apartments, and in doing so, displaced some of our space; this forced us to virtually start over, but we were able to bargain for an extra 5,000 square feet in the process. Our construction costs were initially estimated at US$6.5 million but ultimately reached US$8.5 million. Patricia Smith Melton, a board member, and her husband provided a surprise gift of US$1 million to get us started. The balance came from the D.C. government (US$2.5 million), local and national foundations, private donors, and our board of directors. The D.C. government also provided a property tax abatement (valued at roughly US$50,000 per year) for Woolly Mammoth's portion of the building.

A second piece of advice is this: keep pushing for what you need and at the same time keep reminding everyone of your financial limitations; both messages are necessary. A few more pieces of advice—I cannot help myself:

Invest time in developing a shared vision with your designers. Shortly after we hired McInturff Architects, five of us spent a week in London together—Mark McInturff, his project manager Steve Lawlor, interior specialist Julia Heine, Woolly's technical director Hana Sellers, and myself. We saw plays, toured theaters, met with theater designer Iain MacIntosh, and talked about our project. Many key ideas came from this concentrated time together, including a simple phrase that became the yardstick for our design: "transparent theatrical laboratory." In hindsight, I wish we had invested as much time in developing a relationship with our general contractor.

Think hard before hiring any designer, consultant, or contractor who is working on the base building of which your project is a part. As a rule, you need people who are working just for you. They will need to question the choices of the base building team and fight for changes that will be helpful for your project. In the few cases where we violated this rule we regretted it.

If anything about the design or construction bothers you, say something. No one knows the needs of your organization like you do. In our case, both McInturff and TPC were fantastic to dialogue with, always open to suggestions, and perfectly capable of telling us if they disagreed. The result was a genuine collaboration that constantly moved toward better solutions.

There are a number of things we achieved in the new Woolly Mammoth. The space is breathtaking in its visual impact with an unexpected sense of dimensionality, especially in the open three-tier lobby. The layout is remarkably functional and allows many areas to serve multiple purposes. For example, the rehearsal hall and classroom are beautifully situated off the public lobby to accommodate receptions and small-scale performances.

Our courtyard-style theater retains many of the best features of recent English courtyards, but adds a distinctly American flavor by lowering the stage slightly, tipping up the audience, and introducing lively contrasts of material and color. The stage and seating are flexible within a three-row zone, which lets us transform the configuration at modest cost. Best of all, from the day we moved in, the space felt right, and the entire Woolly family and audience felt at home, despite the much larger scale of our new space.

Working on the project, I learned more than I ever expected to know about theater history, design and construction, but one thing in particular is worth mentioning: there is no finish line. I kept imagining that when we opened for our first performance, we would breathe a sigh of relief and things would settle back to normal. But not only did some construction challenges (like air balancing!) linger for months, but the new pressures of managing the space and producing on a larger scale came rushing at us immediately. Fortunately, our design team continued to be accessible and helpful.

There's a satisfying irony about Woolly Mammoth's award-winning new theater in downtown Washington, D.C. We are a company devoted to new, provocative American plays, some of them critical of our nation's policies, lifestyle, and morality. But we are located not in a marginal neighborhood or converted storefront where one might expect to see such plays. We are located, as of May 2005, in a world-class facility just a stone's throw from the National Archives on some of the most expensive real estate in America.

Woolly is one of a handful of American companies focusing on new plays that have recently graduated to medium-sized, purpose-built theaters. The challenge now is to maintain our risk-taking artistic profile while building the audiences to fill our new venue and sustain our future. The success we've experienced since our move is attributable, in large part, to the tremendous response to our new home. The space is a magnifying glass on our work and inspires us every day to reach new levels of artistic excellence.

Above: Lobby, Woolly Mammoth Theatre

Far left: Theater, Tempe Center for the Arts
Top left: Bar, Tempe Center for the Arts
Left: Lakeside, Tempe Center for the Arts
Above: Lobby, Tempe Center for the Arts

Above and far right: Tempe Center for the Arts
Right: Studio, Tempe Center for the Arts

Left: Dance Studio, '62 Center for Theatre and Dance, Williams College
Above: '62 Center for Theatre and Dance, Williams College

Left and above: MainStage, '62 Center for Theatre and Dance, Williams College
Top: '62 Center for Theatre and Dance, Williams College

All images: CenterStage, '62 Center for Theatre and Dance, Williams College

Holzman Moss Architecture

We believe that architecture must serve a public good by rooting buildings and spaces in their communities, by evoking moments of unexpected joy, and by respecting financial and environmental resources.

Creating distinctive architecture that embodies the singular intent of each project arises out of an exploratory process that thoroughly investigates program needs, existing conditions, material applications, and sustainability. In partnership with our clients, the cultural and physical context of each commission is translated into highly responsive and unique planning and design solutions. The resultant architecture achieves permanence and authenticity while transcending fashion. Our commitment lies in the creation of spaces that inspire. In each a deliberate attempt to incite memorable experiences is found.

Our work celebrates public activity. Specifically in designing, restoring, and expanding theaters, we have focused our attention on creating environments that fire the imagination and enrich the cultural life of local communities. We design facilities for live performance that transport people from the everyday world into special surroundings, where shared experiences and participant interaction are encouraged.

Having completed more than 180 performing arts center projects, we have a thorough understanding that such facilities, to be successful, must be intimate places that foster creative exploration and innovation.

Josh Aisenberg

Daniel Arbelaez

Steve Benesh

Jessica McCormack Blum

Nestor Bottino

Ben Caldwell

Patty Chen

Evan Delli Paoli

Danny Fisher

Sara Francini

Rya Hartman

Jheramis Hernandez

Malcolm Holzman

Eddie Kung

Delia Lewellis

Kevin Morin

Allison Morra

Douglas Moss

Chiun Ng

Nicole Pellegrino

Marilyn Rodriguez

Jennifer Rowe

Cale Sadowski

Connie Tannazzo

Lyna Vuong

Debra Waters

JaffeHolden

At JaffeHolden, productive relationships with our clients and professional colleagues are our most valued assets. With more than four decades of experience, we have learned that our greatest successes occur when relationships are extraordinarily good. We listen carefully to the objectives of our client before commencing design. Then we assign specific people to design unique solutions that couple the client's vision with available resources, thereby ensuring that the results exceed our client's expectations. We apply this methodology to all projects—performing arts, schools and universities, museums, entertainment centers, historic renovations, houses of worship, residential, government, or commercial projects—virtually all facilities that require acoustic, audio, video, technology infrastructure, and/or security consultation services. The JaffeHolden collaborative manner, firmly embedded in our culture, is a defining reason why the facilities we help create are so successful.

JaffeHolden consultants have expertise in acoustics, architecture, touring sound operations, music performance, theatre operations, mechanical and electrical engineering, speaker manufacturing and sales, information technologies, security, and entrepreneurial management. Our team provides the highest quality technical proficiency and sensitivity to every client and every project.

We have state-of-the-art acoustical measurement equipment that allows us to perform acoustic surveys and analysis for all projects. Our acoustic laboratory has a sound isolated semi-anechoic room in which we can test acoustical devices, experiment with the latest acoustical materials, and create acoustical simulations and demonstrations for our clients.

William Armenteros

Courtney Barone

Benjamin Bausher

Michael Cain

Vincenzo Castellano

Mary Cook

Russell Cooper

Sigfrid Hauck

Mark Holden

Jonathan Hopkins

Larry King

Mark Kretchmer

David LaDue

Jonathan Laney

Patricia Neil

Ted Pyper

Lance Ramsey

Mark Reber

Stephanie Resavage

Carlos Rivera

David W. Robb

Michael SantaMaria

Mark Turpin

Oveal Walker

Mark Wilcox

Theatre Projects Consultants

Theatre Projects Consultants creates extraordinary performance spaces around the world. For over 50 years we've provided creative design solutions for our clients on more than 1,000 projects in more than 60 countries. Ranging from small studio theatres to performing arts centers, our projects bring the energy of the art form alive for the audience, artists, and community. But most importantly, we love what we do, and it shows.

We're a team of talented specialists—theatre architects, planners, designers, engineers, and managers. Our team is based in Connecticut and London, with regional offices in Düsseldorf, Shanghai, and Singapore.

We'd like to thank Richard Pilbrow, our founder, for the idea of Theatre Projects Consultants and his countless contributions to the firm.

Carol Allen	John Coyne	Millie Dixon	Jason Osterman
Martin Bailey	Scott Crossfield	Michael D. Ferguson	Richard Pilbrow
Petrus Bertschinger	Marion Daehms	Tony Forman	Stan Pressner
Maggie Casciato	Bert Davis	Keith Gerchak	Czarina Ray
Dawn Chiang	Tom Davis	Jerry Godden	Claire Richards
Jill Collins	Benton Delinger	Rob Gorton	John Riddell
Tom Cousins	Stuart Dingwall	Darren Green	David H. Rosenburg
		Mellodye Green	John Runia
		Leonard Greenwood	Alan Russell
		Andrew Hagan	Mark Ryan
		Brian Hall	Ruth Smallshaw
		Laura Hoff	David Staples
		Tom Lamming	Mark Stroomer
		Jules Lauve III	John I. Tissot
		Oliver Leigers	Rebecca Vincent
		Gene Leitermann	Joseph Volpe
		Kristen Mathias	Lora Warnick
		Ali Mignone	Matt Welander
		Chad Morrison	Matt Young
		Michael Nishball	Ann Zhu

Project data

'62 Center for Theatre and Dance, Williams College

This center provides teaching, performance, and rehearsal spaces for the theater department and dance program. It houses four performance spaces including a 550-seat proscenium theater with seating on three levels, a full stage, and orchestra pit. The studio theater is a flexible space with reconfigurable seating, moveable balconies, and a variable speed, two-level stage lift. The existing theater was renovated into a small, intimate proscenium theater with a large forestage. The center also includes rehearsal spaces for acting, directing, and dance.

Location: Williamstown, Massachusetts, USA **Project type:** New construction and renovation **Completion:** 2005 **Size:** 126,000 gsf
Seating: 550 (Proscenium Theater – MainStage); 220 (Thrust Theater – Adams Memorial Theatre); 200 (Courtyard Theater – CenterStage) Dance Rehearsal Studio **Client:** Williams College **Partners:** Williams College; Williamstown Theatre Festival
Architect: William Rawn Associates **Acoustician:** Acoustic Dimensions **Theater Consultant:** Theatre Projects Consultants

Alice Tully Hall

Alice Tully Hall is one of the most utilized, yet unrecognized, venues at Lincoln Center. Without a major renovation since its opening in 1969, it was badly in need of a transformation. Today the interior of the hall has been re-imagined as a dramatic glowing "vessel" that retains its underlying structural bones. Reshaping of the stage improves on-stage hearing for musicians and more flexibility for theatrical and amplified events.

Location: New York, New York, USA **Project type:** Addition and renovation **Completion:** 2009 **Size:** 242,000 gsf
Seating: 923 to 1,087 **Client:** Lincoln Center **Partners:** Lincoln Center Presents; Great Performances at Lincoln Center; Juilliard School; The Chamber Music Society of Lincoln Center; Film Society of Lincoln Center **Architect:** Diller Scofidio + Renfro **Architect of Record:** FX Fowle **Acoustician:** JaffeHolden **Theater Consultant:** Fisher Dachs Associates

Auditorio Telmex, University of Guadalajara

This multipurpose auditorium has a full stage house and flexibility to support rapid turnarounds for the continuous activity expected from touring shows and local programming. The room can host a variety of audience sizes because of its unique moving sidewalls which reduce the size and seat count of the auditorium while maintaining the same level of intimacy.

Location: Guadalajara, Jalisco, Mexico **Project type:** New construction **Completion:** 2007 **Size:** 330,000 gsf **Seating:** 2,730–10,200 **Client:** La Universidad de Guadalajara **Partners:** The State of Jalisco (Gobierno del Esdato de Jalisco); The City of Zapopan (El Municipio de Zapopan); The University of Guadalajara (La Universidad de Guadalajara); The National Bank of Mexico (El Banco Nacional de México) **Design Architect:** Moyao Arquitectos **Acoustician:** Akustiks **Associate Acoustician:** Cristian Ezcurdia
Theater Design Consultant: Theatre Projects Consultants **Associate Planner:** Arq Alejandro Luna

Aycock Auditorium, University of North Carolina at Greensboro

Since 1927 Aycock Auditorium has served as the nerve center for the University, Greensboro, and the Piedmont Triad region's exuberant performing arts scene. Its renovation preserved the building's historical and noteworthy qualities, improved patron amenities, and modernized the auditorium's systems. A new orchestra pit lift, state-of-the-art audiovisual systems, new theater lighting positions, rigging, and stage equipment were installed. A reconfigured lower level provides space for more performer and production support facilities as well as a new lobby area that connects to the restored gathering space on the main level.

Location: Greensboro, North Carolina, USA **Project type:** Restoration/preservation **Completion:** 2008 **Size:** 62,500 gsf **Seating:** 1,800 **Client:** University of North Carolina, Greensboro **Partners:** UNCG Concert & Lecture Series; Symphonic Band and Wind Ensemble; Symphony Orchestra; Theatre; University Band **Architect:** Gantt Huberman Architects with Holzman Moss Architecture **Acoustician:** Akustiks **Theater Consultant:** Theatre Consultants Collaborative

Benjamin and Marion Schuster Performing Arts Center

Instantly nicknamed the "Schu," the facility offers a wide variety of mixed use including the main multiuse theater, a black box rehearsal space that doubles as a reception room, an 18-story office/condo tower with below grade parking, and a new restaurant. The 2,000 fiber-optic lights in the "dome" of the theater represent the stars in the sky over Dayton the night before the Dayton-based Wright Brothers flew the first airplane.

Location: Dayton, Ohio, USA **Project type:** New construction **Completion:** 2003 **Size:** 168,500 gsf **Seating:** Mead Theater 2,300; Rehearsal Hall 100 **Client:** Arts Center Foundation **Partners:** Dayton Philharmonic, Dayton Opera, Victoria Theater's Broadway touring series **Architect:** Cesar Pelli & Associates **Architect of Record:** GBBN Architects **Acoustician:** JaffeHolden **Theater Consultant:** Theatre Projects Consultants

Center for Contemporary Arts, Shepherd University

The new Center for Contemporary Arts is a joint initiative between Shepherd University and the Contemporary American Theater Festival, a professional, non-profit Equity LORT theater created to realize a shared vision of a building designed to explore and showcase contemporary art and new theater in historic Shepherdstown, the oldest town in the state. The building represents the breaking down of barriers between specializations with the goal of shaping a new center for collaboration and experimentation among performers, playwrights, visual artists, and production designers.

Location: Shepherdstown, West Virginia, USA **Project type:** New construction **Completion:** 2008 **Size:** 104,300 gsf **Seating:** 250 (Thrust Theater, Phase Three); 250 (End-stage Theater, Phase Three); 150 (Studio Theater, Phase Two) **Client:** Contemporary American Theater Festival **Partners:** Shepherd University; Contemporary American Theater Festival **Architect:** Holzman Moss Architecture **Acoustician:** Acoustic Dimensions **Theater Consultant:** Davis Crossfield Associates

Center for the Arts, New Mexico State University

This multiphase complex of structures brings together teaching, performance, and exhibition spaces for the visual arts, music, film and digital arts, theater, and dance. The first phase constructs a new proscenium theater, a large rehearsal room, theater support spaces, classrooms, and faculty offices. A light-filled atrium lobby encourages students, faculty, and community members to gather informally. Inspired by the arroyo, a land formation typical to the New Mexico desert, the atrium's carved path steps back at each level, broadening as it extends toward the sky.

Location: Las Cruces, New Mexico, USA **Project type:** New construction, renovation and adaptive reuse **Completion:** 2011 (Phase One) **Size:** 49,000 gsf (Phase One) **Seating:** 500 (Drama Theater, Phase One); 800 (Multipurpose Hall); 500 (Music Recital Hall); 150 (Flexible Performance Hall) **Client:** New Mexico State University **Partners:** Department of Art; Department of Music; Department of Theatre Arts; Dance Program; Creative Media Institute **Architect:** Holzman Moss Architecture **Associate Architect:** ASA Architects Studio **Acoustician:** Acoustic Dimensions **Theater Consultant:** Theatre Projects Consultants

Center for the Performing Arts, Francis Marion University

This multiuse facility supports a wide variety of programs ranging from university art exhibits and music performances to national touring music, dance, and theater productions. The Center features a mechanized, single-piece, moveable orchestra shell that transforms the stage and fly loft from a tuned musical environment to an open and flexible stagehouse for theatrical events in five minutes. A multistory lobby space connects a black box theater and an academic wing with a rehearsal room, offices, classrooms, and practice rooms. A new lawn creates an outdoor public space that features an amphitheater used for concerts, plays, and community-wide events.

Location: Florence, South Carolina, USA **Project type:** New construction **Completion:** 2010 **Size:** 68,000 gsf **Seating:** 900 (Multipurpose Hall); 100 (Black Box Theater) **Client:** Francis Marion University **Partners:** Francis Marion University; the Bruce & Lee Foundation; State of South Carolina; City of Florence **Architect:** Holzman Moss Architecture **Associate Architect:** FW Architects **Acoustician:** Akustiks **Theater Consultant:** Theatre Consultants Collaborative

Dallas Center for the Performing Arts, Dee and Charles Wyly Theatre

The Dee and Charles Wyly Theatre includes a multiform theater that can be arranged in a variety of configurations including proscenium, thrust, arena, flat floor, and traverse. The 11-story and three-sublevel building features an unprecedented stacked design that rethinks the traditional form of theater.

Location: Dallas, Texas, USA **Project type:** New construction **Completion:** 2009 **Size:** 75,000 gsf **Seating:** 600 **Client:** Dallas Center for the Performing Arts Foundation **Partners:** Dallas Theater Center; Dallas Black Dance; Anita N. Martinez Ballet Folklorico; City of Dallas **Architect:** REX/OMA, Joshua Prince-Ramus (principal in charge) and Rem Koolhaas **Architect of Record:** Kendall/Heaton Associates **Acoustician:** dorsserblesgraaf **Theater Consultant:** Theatre Projects Consultants

Dallas Center for the Performing Arts, Margot and Bill Winspear Opera House

A 21st-century reinterpretation of the traditional "horseshoe" opera house, the Winspear Opera House's principal performance space, the Margaret McDermott Performance Hall, seats 2,200 (with capacity up to 2,300) and features retractable screens, a spacious fly tower, and variable acoustics. The Winspear Opera House also houses the Nancy Hamon Education and Recital Hall, a space that can be used for smaller performances as well as classes, rehearsals, meetings, and events.

Location: Dallas, Texas, USA **Project type:** New construction **Completion:** 2009 **Size:** 198,000 gsf **Seating:** 2,200 (Winspear Opera House); 200 (Nancy Hamon Education and Recital Hall) **Client:** Dallas Center for the Performing Arts Foundation **Partners:** The Dallas Opera; Texas Ballet Theater; City of Dallas **Architect:** Foster and Partners **Architect of Record:** Kendall/Heaton Associates **Acoustician:** Sound Space Design **Theater Consultant:** Theatre Projects Consultants

Doudna Fine Arts Center, Eastern Illinois University

Housing five venues networked together—a concert hall, a proscenium theater, a recital hall, a studio theater, and a lecture hall—are each used for various kinds of presentations. In addition, the center has rehearsal rooms, several corridor art galleries, and practice and teaching studios. The concert hall is enhanced by a new larger and unique, copper-finished orchestra shell allowing musicians to better hear while performing. The recital hall, carved from an old drama theater, has an orchestra shell constructed of glass.

Location: Charleston, Illinois, USA **Project type:** Addition and renovation **Completion:** 2008 **Size:** 234,000 gsf **Seating:** 600 (Dvorak Concert Hall); 250 (Proscenium Theatre); 180 (Recital Hall); 75 (Studio Theatre); 150 (Lecture Hall) **Client:** Eastern Illinois University **Partners:** New and Emerging Artists Series/EIU Foundation; EIU's Tarble Arts Center; EIU's Theater Arts, Music, Art and College of Arts & Humanities Departments **Architect:** Antoine Predock **Architect of Record:** Cannon Design, Chicago, Illinois **Acoustician:** JaffeHolden **Theater Consultant:** Schuler Shook

The Eli and Edythe Broad Stage, Santa Monica College

The Eli and Edythe Broad Stage is unique in providing the intimate immediacy of a 499-seat hall yet with a variable proscenium and a stage able to accommodate a full orchestra. Its 99-seat, flexible, smaller rehearsal hall is used for the presentation of spontaneous and experimental works as well as other types of performance.

Location: Santa Monica, California, USA **Project type:** Addition **Completion:** 2008 **Size:** 30,000 gsf **Seating:** 499 (Broad Stage); 99 (The Edye Second Space) **Client:** Santa Monica College **Partners:** Dustin Hoffman; Dale Franzen; Santa Monica Community College; Dr. Chui Tsang **Architect:** Renzo Zecchetto **Acoustician:** JaffeHolden **Theater Consultant:** Fisher Dachs Associates

Esplanade – Theatres on the Bay

One of the most important performing arts complexes in Asia, this center promotes multicultural exchange between Eastern and Western cultures. The concert hall features adjustable acoustics to accommodate a wide range of music. The horseshoe-shaped multipurpose theater has an adjustable proscenium and orchestra pit and can accommodate drama, dance, and opera.

Location: Singapore **Project type:** New construction **Completion:** 2002 **Size:** 291,000 gsf **Seating:** 2,000 (Multipurpose Hall); 1,600 (Concert Hall); 245 (Recital Hall); 220 (Studio Theater); Outdoor Theater **Client:** Ministry of Information, Communications and the Arts **Partners:** The Esplanade Company Ltd.; Ministry of Information, Communications and the Arts **Architect:** Michael Wilford & Partners **Associate Architect:** DP Architects **Acoustician:** Artec Consultants **Theater Consultant:** Theatre Projects Consultants

George A. Purefoy Municipal Center

The George A. Purefoy Municipal Center alludes to the tradition of Texas courthouses overlooking a public green site while incorporating the latest technologies in energy-efficient design. By creating a partnership between two institutions, the library has been able to make use of City Hall spaces, such as the Council Chamber, for performances, ceremonies, and celebrations and both have shared access to meeting rooms, a café, and a gallery.

Location: Frisco, Texas, USA **Project type:** New construction **Completion:** 2006 **Size:** 150,000 gsf **Seating:** 300 (Council Chamber) **Client:** City of Frisco **Partners:** Frisco Public Library; Frisco City Hall **Architect:** Holzman Moss Architecture **Acoustician:** Acoustic Dimensions **Theater Consultant:** Davis Crossfield Associates

Globe-News Center for the Performing Arts

A community venue near historic Route 66, the Globe-News Center for the Performing Arts is used by the local orchestra, ballet, opera, and other regional arts organizations, as well as touring companies. At its heart is a multipurpose auditorium distinguished by a one-of-a-kind design. Its single-piece reflective orchestra shell moves on and off stage via hand-held, wireless remote control, transforming the auditorium from a concert hall into a theater, in less than four minutes.

Location: Amarillo, Texas, USA **Project type:** New construction **Completion:** 2006 **Size:** 71,000 gsf **Seating:** 1,250 **Client:** City of Amarillo, Texas **Partners:** The Amarillo Symphony; Amarillo Opera; Lone Star Ballet **Architect:** Holzman Moss Architecture **Acoustician:** JaffeHolden **Theater Consultant:** Davis Crossfield Associates

Hylton Performing Arts Center, George Mason University

The Hylton Performing Arts Center expands the reach and opportunities of the University's School of Fine Arts; enhances the lives of City of Manassas residents; and supports the development of Prince William County as a distinct and attractive place to live, work, and visit. Its four-level, opera-style multipurpose auditorium is a facility for academic, regional, and national events as well as a permanent home to such local entities as the Prince William Symphony Orchestra and the Bull Run Cloggers.

Location: Manassas, Virginia, USA **Project type:** New construction **Completion:** 2010 **Size:** 92,700 gsf **Seating:** 1,166 (Multipurpose Hall); 277 (Black Box Theater); 106 (Rehearsal Room) **Client:** George Mason University **Partners:** George Mason University; City of Manassas, Virginia; Prince William County **Architect:** Holzman Moss Architecture **Architect of Record:** Hughes Group Architects **Acoustician:** BAi, LLC **Theater Consultant:** Davis Crossfield Associates

ImaginOn: The Joe & Joan Martin Center

By joining together the Children's Theatre of Charlotte and the youth services division of the Public Library of Charlotte Mecklenburg County, ImaginOn creates the opportunity for engagement with stories in a manner unlike any before. An integrated part of Charlotte's expanding uptown arts district, the building is intended to stir the imagination. Forms such as a parallelogram, a helix, and a cube, along with materials, colors, and textures are all open to interpretation just as any element of a story might be.

Location: Charlotte, North Carolina, USA **Project type:** New construction **Completion:** 2005 **Size:** 114,000 gsf **Seating:** 550 (McColl Family Theatre); 250 (Wachovia Playhouse); 60 (Storytelling Room) **Client:** Public Library of Charlotte & Mecklenburg County **Partners:** Public Library of Charlotte Mecklenburg County; Children's Theatre of Charlotte **Architect:** Gantt Huberman Architects with Holzman Moss Architecture **Acoustician:** JaffeHolden **Theater Consultant:** Theatre Projects Consultants

The Institute of Contemporary Art

The Institute of Contemporary Art (ICA) is a dramatic cantilevered form enfolding more than 65,000 square feet of space dedicated exclusively to acquiring and exhibiting contemporary art. Views of Boston Harbor become the backdrop to its new theater, which allows ICA to expand its offerings in the performing arts and film genres. Located under Logan Airport's flight path, the theater, with its two glass walls, demanded integrated acoustic systems for sound quality control and special sound attenuating glazing systems.

Location: Boston, Massachusetts, USA **Project type:** New construction **Completion:** 2006 **Size:** 65,000 gsf **Seating:** 325 **Client:** Institute of Contemporary Art **Partners:** Boston Redevelopment Authority; Institute of Contemporary Art **Architect:** Diller Scofidio & Renfro **Architect of Record:** Perry Dean Rogers & Partners **Acoustician:** JaffeHolden **Theater Consultant:** Fisher Dachs Associates

Joe R. and Teresa Long Center for the Performing Arts

The two venues, Dell Hall and the Rollins Theatre, support clear, sharp, natural acoustics for performances of the founding resident companies: the Austin Symphony Orchestra, Austin Lyric Opera, and Ballet Austin, as well as many other community arts groups. The acoustics are adjustable and "tunable" to keep amplified events from being too loud and coarse for listeners. The Long Center hosts multiple events at once; its venues are designed to isolate sound in adjacent spaces.

Location: Austin, Texas, USA **Project type:** Adaptive reuse **Completion:** 2008 **Size:** 235,000 gsf **Seating:** 2,310 (Multipurpose Hall); 150 (Flexible Theater) **Client:** ARTS Center Stage **Partners:** Austin Symphony Orchestra, Austin Lyric Opera, and Ballet Austin **Architect:** Nelsen Partners/Zeidler Partnership Architects **Acoustician:** JaffeHolden **Theater Consultant:** Fisher Dachs Associates

Kansas City Music Hall

One of the finest art deco masterpieces since Radio City Music Hall in New York City, the Kansas City Music Hall is an extraordinary structure that was completed in 1936. The renovation and expansion project includes a substantial amount of work that occurs "behind the scenes" in the backstage, back-of-house, and support areas. The stagehouse extension is clad in undulating stainless steel panels inspired by the scalloped-shaped stone defining the cornice of the building.

Location: Kansas City, Missouri, USA **Project type:** Addition and renovation **Completion:** 2007 **Size:** 20,000 gsf **Seating:** 2,400 **Client:** City of Kansas City **Partners:** Kansas City Symphony; Kansas City Ballet; Broadway Touring Shows (Broadway Across America) **Architect:** Holzman Moss Architecture **Associate Architect:** Helix Architecture + Design, Inc. **Acoustician:** TALASKE **Theater Consultant:** Fisher Dachs Associates

Marion Oliver McCaw Hall at Seattle Center

A major criterion for the renovation of the Opera House, renamed the Marion Oliver McCaw Hall, was to preserve the hall's well-respected acoustics for opera and ballet productions. McCaw Hall now has the vocal richness and clarity of the original, while creating a more acoustically intimate connection between performers and audience. A new sound reinforcement system meets the needs of the community festivals, theater, poetry, and other events. A 288-seat hall, specifically designed for pre-performance lectures, has been added to the complex.

Location: Seattle, Washington, USA **Project type:** Addition and renovation **Completion:** 2003 **Size:** 280,000 gsf **Seating:** 2,900 (Marion Oliver McCaw Hall); 288 (Lecture Hall) **Client:** Seattle Center **Partners:** Seattle Opera; Pacific Northwest Ballet **Architect:** LMN Architects **Acoustician:** JaffeHolden **Associate Acoustician:** Michael Yantis and Associates **Theater Consultant:** Schuler Shook

Moores School of Music, University of Houston

The Moores Opera House is a "jewel box" theater that can accommodate the full range of student productions—operas, symphony orchestra concerts, jazz ensembles, and popular music events. Outfitted with a full stagehouse, orchestra pit, orchestra shell, variable acoustics, and a state-of-the-art sound system, the hall lets student performers experience creating music in a true concert environment—one that is acoustically accurate and quickly responsive to sound sources. The building also houses rehearsal rooms, practice rooms, studios, and classrooms.

Location: Houston, Texas, USA **Project type:** New construction **Completion:** 1997 **Size:** 300,000 gsf **Seating:** 800 **Client:** University of Houston **Partners:** Houston Grand Opera; University of Houston's Opera Department, Symphonic, Wind, Jazz and Chamber Music Ensembles and Faculty **Architect:** The Mathes Group **Acoustician:** JaffeHolden **Theater Consultant:** Theatre Projects Consultants

The Music Center at Strathmore

Designed to high acoustic standards, the concert hall has a wide range of open staging capabilities that can accommodate everything from acoustic performances, popular music, and dance presentations. It is the second home for the Baltimore Symphony Orchestra. Part of The Music Center complex includes an arts education center with classrooms and rehearsal space for music, dance, and theater. The center is a vital part of bringing art to the belt communities outside of Washington, DC.

Location: North Bethesda, Maryland, USA **Project type:** New construction **Completion:** 2005 **Size:** 190,000 gsf **Seating:** 2,000 **Client:** Strathmore **Partners:** Baltimore Symphony Orchestra at Strathmore; National Philharmonic; Washington Performing Arts Society; Levine School of Music; CityDance Center; Maryland Classic Youth Orchestra; InterPlay **Architect:** William Rawn Associates **Associate Architect:** Grimm + Parker Architects **Acoustician:** Kirkegaard Associates **Theater Consultant:** Theatre Projects Consultants

Nancy Lee and Perry R. Bass Performance Hall

As flexible as it is virtuosic, JaffeHolden's Concert Hall Shaper converts Bass Hall into an intimate performance space for the Dallas/Fort Worth Ballet and the Fort Worth Opera. With the Shaper stored out of the way high on the backstage wall, line sets are unimpeded, and the adjustable orchestra pit can be reconfigured to accommodate ensembles of different sizes, ranging up to 100 musicians. To serve the needs of touring Broadway musicals and other popular performances, the hall is outfitted with a state-of-the-art sound reinforcement system.

Location: Fort Worth, Texas, USA **Project type:** New construction **Completion:** 1998 **Size:** 180,000 gsf **Seating:** 2052 **Client:** Performing Arts, Fort Worth **Partners:** Dallas/Fort Worth Ballet, Fort Worth Opera **Architect:** David M. Schwartz Architects **Acoustician:** JaffeHolden **Theater Consultant:** Fisher Dachs Associates

New World Symphony

The New World Symphony is a unique educational environment that prepares gifted graduates of distinguished music programs for leadership positions in orchestra and ensembles around the world. The new building is designed to expand and support its extensive distance learning capabilities by integrating Internet2 technology (a broadband network 100,000 times faster than the internet), 360-degree video projection, advanced video, and audio streaming and recording into a building-wide system that allows worldwide connectivity.

Location: Miami Beach, Florida, USA **Project type:** New construction **Completion:** 2010 **Size:** 106,500 gsf **Seating:** 700 (Interactive Concert Hall); 150 (Interactive/Multipurpose Room); Multiple practice rooms and ensemble rehearsal rooms **Client:** New World Symphony **Partners:** New World Symphony; City of Miami Beach **Architect:** Gehry Partners **Acoustician:** Nagata Acoustics **Theater Consultant:** Theatre Projects Consultants

The New York Times Center

In the heart of this new home for The New York Times, a new state-of-the-art performance space, The Times Center, is provided for multiple uses, ranging from simple lecture presentations to musical and theatrical performances. Electronic architecture provides the full range of variability needed to take the relatively dry natural signature of the room and smoothly fill in the diffuse energy needed for chamber music.

Location: New York, New York, USA **Project type:** New construction **Completion:** 2007 **Size:** 5,000 gsf **Seating:** 378 **Client:** The New York Times **Partners:** The New York Times; New York Times Live; TimesTalks; The Center for Creative Resources **Architect:** Renzo Piano Building Workshop **Architect of Record:** Fox Fowle Architects **Developer:** Forest City Ratner Companies **Acoustician:** JaffeHolden **Theater Consultant:** Fisher Dachs Associates

Oslo Opera House

This new home for the Den Norske Opera & Ballet was constructed by the Norwegian Government on the waterfront in the capital, Oslo. The 600-member opera and ballet company has been provided with a 1,400-seat main house and a 400-seat experimental theater, together with extensive production facilities. Capital financing was from North Sea oil revenues.

Location: Oslo, Norway **Project type:** New construction **Completion:** 2008 **Size:** 414,400 gsf **Seating:** 1,400 (Opera House); 400 (Experimental Theatre); 200 (Rehearsal Stage) **Client:** Statsbygg **Partners:** Ministry of Culture and Church Affairs; Ministry of Government Administration and Reform; The Norwegian Opera & Ballet **Architect:** Snøhetta **Acoustician:** Brekke Strand Arup **Theater Consultant:** Theatre Projects Consultants

Overture Center for the Arts

The center is the result of the renovation and expansion of the Madison Civic Center by a partnership of the Overture Foundation and the City of Madison. The project was completely funded by the Foundation and incorporates new, renovated, and rehabilitated performance venues as well as new galleries for the Madison Museum of Contemporary Art and the Wisconsin Academy of Sciences, Arts, and Letters.

Location: Madison, Wisconsin, USA **Project type:** New construction, addition and renovation, and adaptive reuse **Completion:** 2006 **Size:** 400,000 gsf **Seating:** 2,250 (Overture Hall); 1,000 (Capitol Theater); 350 (The Playhouse); 200 (Rotunda Stage); 200 (Promenade Hall) **Client:** Overture Development Corporation **Partners:** Overture Foundation; City of Madison; Madison Cultural Arts District; Madison Symphony Orchestra; Madison Opera; Madison Ballet; Madison Repertory Theatre; Wisconsin Chamber Orchestra; Kanopy Dance **Architect:** Pelli Clarke Pelli Architects **Architect of Record:** Potter Lawson & Flad Architects **Acoustician:** Kirkegaard Associates **Theater Consultant:** Theatre Projects Consultants

Palais Montcalm

Seventy-five years after it was founded, the Palais Montcalm has been reborn and reinvented into a venue for artists representing a wide variety of musical genres ranging in style from traditional to contemporary. The Salle Raoul Jobin is a 979-seat concert hall with exceptional acoustics. Café-spectacles, a completely modular multipurpose facility, doubles as a rehearsal and performance space for up-and-coming performers, emerging music, and smaller ensembles. Other amenities include a recording studio, a coffee bar, and administrative offices.

Location: Quebec, Canada **Project type:** Renovation **Completion:** 2007 **Size:** 48,000 gsf **Seating:** 979 (Concert Hall); 125 (Rehearsal Hall) **Client:** City of Quebec **Partners:** Les Violonsdu Roy; Société lyrique d'Aubigny **Architect:** Bernard & Cloutier; St. Gelais Montiminy; Jacques Plante Architecte **Architect of Record:** M.U.S.E., a consortium of the three above-named firms **Acoustician:** JaffeHolden **Theater Consultant:** Go Multimedia

Performance Hall – Crocus International – Expo 3

This 6,000-seat performance hall will be the largest privately owned, public presentation and gathering facility in Moscow, accommodating a range of performances including rock concerts, symphonic concerts, ballets, theatrical presentations, conferences, and more. Aiming to wow, the developer desires a one-of-a-kind interior space, making it the venue of choice for performers and audiences alike.

Location: Moscow, Russian Federation **Project type:** New construction **Completion:** 2009 (estimated) **Size:** 157,000 gsf **Seating:** 6,000 **Client:** Crocus International **Architect:** Holzman Moss Architecture **Acoustician:** JaffeHolden **Theater Consultant:** Davis Crossfield Associates

Performing Arts Center, Texas A&M University-Corpus Christi

The new Performing Arts Center reflects the university's commitment to cultivating new curricula in the performing arts and enhancing the cultural environment on campus, Corpus Christi, and the south Texas region. In Phase 1—a 1,510-seat concert hall—provides a venue for a wide variety of student and professional performances. The concert hall volume is rotated on the orthogonal to reveal vistas of Corpus Christi Bay from the multistoried public areas.

Location: Corpus Christi, Texas, USA **Project type:** New construction **Completion:** 2005 **Size:** 55,000 gsf **Seating:** 1,510 (Concert Hall, Phase One); 500 (Theater, Phase Two) **Client:** Texas A&M University-Corpus Christi **Partners:** Texas A&M University-Corpus Christi; Corpus Christi Symphony Orchestra **Architect:** Holzman Moss Architecture **Architect of Record:** Cotten Landreth Kramer Architects & Associates **Acoustician:** JaffeHolden **Theater Consultant:** Fisher Dachs Associates

Plano Courtyard Theater

The 325-seat theater provides an environment for performances by local organizations, the Plano Independent School District, and the Plano Symphony Orchestra, as well as touring groups. The theater and lobby spaces are housed within the original Cox Gymnasium, taking advantage of its larger interior spaces while bringing new life to this well-known 1935 community building. The theater can be arranged to allow frontal, thrust, or theater-in-the-round style presentations, which allows transformation into a flexible performance space.

Location: Plano, Texas, USA **Project type:** Renovation/reuse **Completion:** 2002 **Size:** 22,500 gsf **Seating:** 325 **Client:** City of Plano, Texas **Partners:** City of Plano; Plano Independent School District **Architect:** Hardy Holzman Pfeiffer Associates **Acoustician:** JaffeHolden **Theater Consultant:** Theatre Projects Consultants

RiverCenter for the Performing Arts

A thriving, downtown cultural center for the citizens of Columbus and its university community, RiverCenter for the Performing Arts features multiple halls which meet a wide range of performance needs from Broadway shows, symphonic concerts, dance performances, and pop concerts, to lectures and conferences. Integrating professional and educational spaces, the facility also includes classrooms, studios, rehearsal rooms, and practice rooms for Columbus State University's Schwob School of Music.

Location: Columbus, Georgia, USA **Project type:** New construction **Completion:** 2002 **Size:** 246,000 gsf **Seating:** 2,000 (Multiple-use-hall Bill Heard Theater); 450 (Legacy Hall); 150 (Studio/Theater/Chamber Hall) **Client:** River Center for the Performing Arts **Partners:** Downtown Development Authority of Columbus; the Georgia Attorney General's Office; the Board of Regents of the State University System **Architect:** Hardy Holzman Pfeiffer Associates **Architect of Record:** Hecht Burdeshaw, Johnson, Kidd and Clark **Acoustician:** JaffeHolden **Theater Consultant:** Theatre Projects Consultants

Roe Green Center, Kent State University

The Roe Green Center unifies the Departments of Theatre and Dance under one roof in a series of new additions to the Music and Speech Building. A black box theater, dance studios, and a grand lobby in addition to renovation and remodeling provide state-of-the-art production facilities and studios. The new lobby affords the building greater prominence as visitors arrive and connects the black box theater to an existing 500-seat theater.

Location: Kent, Ohio, USA **Project type:** Addition and renovation **Completion:** 2010 **Size:** 46,400 gsf (new), 32,200 gsf (renovation) **Seating:** 200 (Black Box Theater) **Client:** Kent State University **Partners:** Hugh A. Glauser School of Music; School of Theatre and Dance **Architect:** Holzman Moss Architecture **Associate Architect:** GPD Group **Acoustician:** BAi **Theater Consultant:** Davis Crossfield Associates

Roundhouse

Built in 1847 as a steam engine turning shed, and later converted to a bonded warehouse and then an arts venue, the Roundhouse has played host to many influential performances. The Roundhouse reopened in 2006 following an extensive refurbishment that retained and restored many of the original features, creating a modern and fully accessible facility dedicated to nurturing creative young talent, as well as presenting an eclectic line-up of the best in live music, theater, dance, and circus.

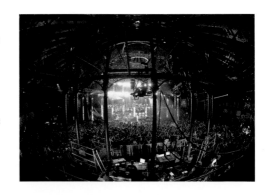

Location: London, United Kingdom **Project type:** Renovation **Completion:** 2006 **Size:** 71,000 gsf **Seating:** 1,800 (Main Space); 150 (Dr. Martens FREEDM Studio) **Client:** Roundhouse Trust **Partners:** Camden Council; Arts Council England; Department for Education and Skills; London Development Agency; Latham & Watkins; Heritage Lottery Fund; The Norman Trust; The Paul Hamlyn Foundation; The Wellcome Trust; Garfield Weston Foundation; Stuart Wheeler **Architect:** John McAslan & Partners **Acoustician:** Paul Gillieron Acoustic Design **Theater Consultant:** Theatre Projects Consultants

The Sage Gateshead

This center, which presents music from all over the world, consists of a 1,750-seat concert hall, a 450-seat flexible performance space, and a large rehearsal space, all with world-class acoustics, and a 26-room Music Education Center. Of equal importance to the varied performance program is the center's educational work, the largest music education program by a single institution anywhere in the world, which strives to encourage people from all walks of life to develop their musical capabilities, either by traditional academic qualifications or more vocational outreach programs.

Location: Gateshead, Tyne and Wear, United Kingdom **Project type:** New construction **Completion:** 2004 **Size:** 188,500 gsf **Seating:**1,750 (Concert Hall); 450 (Flexible Theater) **Client:** Gateshead Council and North Music Trust **Partners:** Northern Sinfonia; Folkworks (now incorporated into the unique management structure of North Music Trust) **Architect:** Foster + Partners **Acoustician:** Arup Acoustics **Theater Consultant:** Theatre Projects Consultants

School of American Ballet

The School of American Ballet is part of the official training academy for the New York City Ballet. The addition includes two new dance studios stacked within the space of the two existing dance studios. A unique custom double-glazed system allows full transparency on three walls, floor to ceiling, yet blocks all sound between adjoining studios. Custom, fully glazed acoustic doors and acoustic ceilings are completely smooth and cannot be distinguished from the plaster.

Location: New York, New York, USA **Project type:** Renovation **Completion:** 2007 **Size:** 8,200 **Client:** Lincoln Center **Partners:** New York City Ballet; Lincoln Center **Architect:** Diller Scofidio + Renfro **Acoustician:** JaffeHolden

Student Union Building, Texas Tech University

Renovation and expansion of the Student Union Building encourages users to congregate with its assortment of scaled spaces that accommodate individuals and groups of all sizes for study, presentation, socializing, and recreation. The Allen Theater and a new 100-seat theater are used for lectures, art films, and special events that augment other activities.

Location: Lubbock, Texas, USA **Project type:** New construction and renovation **Completion:** 2006 **Size:** 95,250 gsf (new), 80,000 gsf (renovation) **Seating:** 968 (Allen Theater); 100 (Small Theater) **Client:** Texas Tech University **Architect:** Holzman Moss Architecture **Acoustician:** BAi, LLC

Sun Valley Pavilion

The Sun Valley Music Pavilion is a structure with clear sight lines, all naturally integrated into a spectacular site. Natural acoustics are complemented by an integrated audio and video system that combines both a touring show-ready audio system inside the pavilion with a distributed audio system for the lawn seating. The high-tech shell is formed of a seasonal tensile membrane to provide a luminous reflective space and a permanent wood-shingled roof for acoustic blending.

Location: Sun Valley, Idaho, USA **Project type:** New construction **Completion:** 2008 **Size:** 48,000 gsf **Seating:** 1,500 (Permanent); 3,500 (Lawn) **Client:** Sun Valley Company **Partners:** Sun Valley Symphony; Sun Valley Company **Architect:** FTL Design Engineering Studio, New York **Architect of Record:** Ruscitto/Latham/Blanton Architects **Acoustician:** JaffeHolden **Theater Consultant:** Auerbach Pollack Friedlander

Tempe Center for the Arts

Located within a 17-acre art park on the banks of Tempe's Town Lake, the building's monolithic roof form encloses a multistory interior "street" on which the performance venues and an art gallery sit as distinct building forms. The public spaces incorporate several public art pieces and offer striking views of the Rio Salado and nearby Papago Mountains.

Location: Tempe, Arizona, USA **Project type:** New construction **Completion:** 2007 **Size:** 80,000 gsf **Seating:** 600 (Proscenium Theater); 200 (Flexible Studio Theater) **Client:** City of Tempe **Partners:** Tempe Symphony Orchestra; Tempe Little Theatre; Childsplay; Desert Dance Theater; A Ludwig Dance Theatre; Tempe Municipal Arts Commission; Arizona Academy of the Performing Arts; Tempe Community Chorus; Local Visual Artists **Architect:** Barton Myers Associates and Architekton **Acoustician:** ARUP Acoustics **Theater Consultant:** Theatre Projects Consultants

Tokyo International Forum

Hall C in the Tokyo International Forum is a 1,500-seat theater that can be configured to serve a broad range of needs from symphonic performances to drama and is acoustically adjusted to precisely match the needs of each. For symphonic events, a concert ceiling is lowered in the stage house to seal off the fly tower and its sound-absorbing scenery and drapery. This ceiling creates a resonant chamber around the orchestra resulting in a very rich and warm acoustic. Suspended below is a lower acoustical canopy which ensures that this resonance is balanced by clarity and transparency. For dance, opera, and other performances, the canopy and concert ceiling fold away to allow unrestricted access to the fully rigged stagehouse.

Location: Tokyo, Japan **Project type:** New construction **Completion:** 1996 **Size:** 19,700 gsf **Seating:** 1,500 (Opera/Drama/Symphony Hall); 5,000 (Multipurpose Hall) **Client:** Tokyo Municipal Government **Partners:** Opera; Drama; Symphony; Municipality **Architect:** Rafael Viñoly **Acoustician:** JaffeHolden **Associate Acoustician:** Yamaha Acoustic Research Labs **Theater Consultant:** Fisher Dachs Associates, Theater Workshop

Unicorn Children's Centre

The Unicorn is an inspirational flagship center in the United Kingdom aiming to move theater for children into a contemporary frame. Its ambition is to provide the highest quality professional theater for children in a stimulating environment, complementing this by an enterprising educational program. The Unicorn Theatre includes two theaters, rehearsal rooms, and an education center.

Location: London, United Kingdom **Project type:** New construction **Completion:** 2005 **Size:** 39,200 gsf **Seating:** 340 (Weston Theatre); 120 (Clore Theatre) **Client:** Unicorn Children's Centre Ltd. **Partners:** Unicorn Children's Centre; Caryl Jenner Productions/Unicorn Theatre for Children; Arts Council England – National Lottery Funding **Architect:** Keith Williams Architects **Acoustician:** Arup Acoustics **Theater Consultant:** Theatre Projects Consultants

Woolly Mammoth Theatre

This new facility designed for the innovative repertory company houses a flexible courtyard theater which can be configured in either endstage or small thrust configurations. The theater is located within a new development in mid-town Washington, D.C. and sports a two-tiered lobby and two cafés.

Location: Washington, D.C., USA **Project type:** New construction, fit-out in a commercial development **Completion:** 2005 **Size:** 32,000 gsf **Seating:** 265 **Client:** Woolly Mammoth Theatre Company **Partners:** Woolly Mammoth Theatre Company; District of Columbia; JPI Development **Architect:** McInturff Architects **Acoustician:** Acoustic Dimensions **Theater Consultant:** Theatre Projects Consultants

Acknowledgments

230

The rich compendium of projects illustrated in *Theaters 2* is testament to the power of partnerships in producing dynamic facilities for the performing arts that enrich the cultural lives of their communities. The success of each is fully dependent on the potential of all professionals involved in the planning, design, and construction process to be active and enthusiastic collaborators. The individuals, clients, and firms who have contributed their creative energies and insights on these projects are many, and we are thankful to them for their meaningful contributions.

We are especially grateful to The Images Publishing Group's publishers, Paul Latham and Alessina Brooks, who proposed a second volume to Theaters in recognition of the continued importance of this topic on an international level. Editor, Andrew Hall, deserves credit for keeping up with us as projects and layouts continued to evolve.

It is particularly fortunate to have Jessica McCormack Blum at the helm of this effort. Jessica, having spearheaded photography for *Theaters*, brought the same perseverance to bear in assembling *Theaters 2*; she is expert in the tumultuous exercise of coordinating photography and essays. A second stroke of luck was having Debra Waters write the Introduction, as she had done previously for *Theaters*, and serving as our discerning in-house editor.

Additionally, we would like to give special thanks to Courtney Barone, Russ Cooper, John Coyne, Keith Gerchak, Kristen Mathias, Kevin Moran, Chad Morrison, and Ruth Smallshaw, whose efforts embellish each page of our book.

Holzman Moss Architecture, JaffeHolden, and Theatre Projects Consultants would like to acknowledge past employees who dedicated their skill and imagination to the projects in this publication:

Cleveland Adams
Cy Almey
Robert Almodovar
Niklas Anderson
Ben Ardwin
Fermin Beltran
Kristin Blake
Sam Brandt
James Breeds
Richard Bunn
Elisabeth Bury
Ryan Bussard
Michael Connolly
Brian Corry
Albert Debnam
Liz Diaz
George Ellerington
Jayme Elterman
Elizabeth Evans
Jamie Feuerborn
Padraic Fisher
Louis Fleming
Andrew Gardner
Jean Gath
Elissa Getto
Robin Glosemeyer
Victor Gotesman
Gavin Green

Hugh Hardy
Darwin Harrison
Andrei Harwell
Steve Hass
Andy Hayles
Clare Hurtgen
Chris Jaffe
Matt Jasmin
Christopher Kaiser
Astrid Kirchholtes
Matthew Kirschner
Bob Kronman
Alison Lee
Rob Lilkendey
Ching-Wen Lin
Robert Long
John Lui
Bradley Lukanic
Iain Mackintosh
Giancarlo Massaro
Sheila McAuliffe
Karen McInerney
Anne Minors
Robert Naybour
Jim Niesel
Mindy No
Ryoko Okada
Michael Patterson

Norman Pfeiffer
Daria Pizzetta
Andrea Pratt
Jose Reyes
Jae Rhee
Howard Rose
Paul Scarbrough
Jerome Smith
Allan Smith
Laurence Southon
Tony Stafford
Jon Stevens
Margaret Sullivan
Steve Sweet
Michael Taylor
David Taylor
Jack Tilbury
Russ Todd
Ian Tomkinson
Jose Torres
Martin Trumpf
David Tye
John Viesta
Binita Vijayvergiya
Janne Woltmann
Robert Young
Athos Zaghi

Photography credits

© 2008 Len Allington 17 (top), 42–43, 44 (top right, bottom), 45, 84–85, 86–87, 89, 129, 221 (bottom right), 223 (bottom right), 225 (top left)

© 2008 Matthew Arnold Photography 136–137, 225 (bottom left)

© 2009 Anacleto Rapping 178–179, 180 (bottom left), 181

© Aker/Zvonkovic 158–159, 159, 160–161, 224 (bottom right)

Allover Norway/Rex Features 114–115, 225 (bottom right)

Amanda Rose Photography 168–169, 169 (top right)

Amarillo Globe-News, Photo by Michael Schumacher 15

© Andy Snow 102–103, 104, 105, 220 (top left)

Arcaid/Richard Bryant 150–151, 153, 228 (top right)

© Bass Performance Hall, Rodger Mallison 128

BBC Electric Proms 2007, courtesy Roundhouse 169 (bottom right), 227 (bottom right)

Ben Rudick 214 (top)

Benny Chan 179 (right), 180 (top left), 222 (top right)

© benoit.lafrance@yahoo.ca 148, 149, 226 (top left)

Courtesy Callas Contractors, Inc. 177 (bottom)

Christine Simmons Portraiture 6 (Benton Delinger)

Courtesy City of Frisco, Texas 82–83 (bottom)

© Craig Blackmon, FAIA 130–131, 131 (top), 132, 134, 135 (right), 227 (top left)

© Darwin Harrison 82–83 (top), 133

© Debra Waters 100 (bottom right)

© Donna Bise 9 (top), 60–61 (top)

© Donna Pallotta 18 (bottom)

© Doug Fitch 79

© Douglas Moss 12

Foster + Partners 32 (bottom), 32–33, 34 (top), 221 (bottom left)

© FTL Design Engineering Studio 185 (bottom)

Gehry Partners, courtesy New World Symphony 146–147, 225 (top right)

Hélène Binet 192–193, 194, 195, 229 (bottom left)

Hester & Hardaway Photographers 9 (bottom), 196, 198, 199, 226 (bottom left)

Hidetaki Mori 55, 57 (top right), 59

©Holzman Moss Architecture 13

Courtesy Holzman Moss Architecture, rendering by Daniel Barrenechea 120–121 (bottom), 121 (top), 170–171, 220 (bottom left), 226 (bottom right)

Courtesy Holzman Moss Architecture, rendering by Lee Dunnette, AIA 91

Courtesy Holzman Moss Architecture, rendering by Studio AMD 36–37, 38, 39, 40, 70–71, 98–99, 221 (top left), 223 (top left), 227 (bottom left)

Hufton + Crow 169 (top right)

© Iwan Baan 19, 26–27, 28, 29, 30, 31, 72–73, 74–75, 76–77, 78, 162–163, 164–165, 167, 219 (middle), 223 (bottom left), 228 (top left)

© James Steinkamp, Steinkamp Photography 44 (top left)

Jaro Hollan, Statsbygg 110, 111, 112–113

© Jeff Goldberg/Esto 18 (top)

© Jeff Goldberg/Esto, Pelli Clarke Pelli 122–123, 124, 126–127, 226 (top right)

Jeff Janko, Texas A&M University-Corpus Christi 11 (bottom), 197 (left)

© Jeremy Blaine 172–173, 175 (top), 176

© Jim Cawthorne, Camera 1 140, 141 (bottom), 142

John Edward Linden 207 (right), 208, 209, 229 (top left)

© Jonathan Hillyer Photography, Inc. 21, 138–139, 141 (top), 145, 227 (top right)

Julia Heine, McInturff Architects 200, 201, 202, 203 (bottom), 205, 229 (bottom right)

© Kris Berg 182–183, 186–187

© Lara Swimmer Photography 94–95, 96, 97, 224 (top left)

© Long Center for the Performing Arts 17 (bottom)

Luxigon 32 (top), 34 (bottom), 35, 221 (top right)

© Malcolm Holzman 11 (top left), 177 (top)

© Meg Carlough 121 (right)

Michael Masengarb/Architekton 206, 207 (top)

Nigel Young, courtesy Foster + Partners 154, 156–157

Nina Reistad 108–109

Paul Gordon Emerson/CityDance Ensemble featuring dancer Alice Wylie 107 (bottom)

© Paul Pape, 2004 11 (top right)

Richard Barnes 25

Robert Benson Photography 210, 211, 212, 213, 214 (bottom), 215, 219 (top)

Ron Solomon 106–107, 107 (top) 224 (bottom left)

Courtesy Roundhouse 169 (top left)

Rubén Orozco 69 (top)

© Russell Reed 131 (bottom), 135 (left)

Sally Ann Norman Photography 24 (bottom)

Schwartz/Silver Architects 23 (top)

© Sun Valley Pavilion, Mary Elizabeth Cook 185 (top), 228 (bottom left)

©The Image Collection, University Archive & Manuscripts, The University of North Carolina at Greensboro 118 (top, bottom)

Theatre Projects 68–69, 69 (bottom), 125, 203 (top), 207 (bottom), 219 (bottom)

Tim Griffith 24 (top), 54–55, 56, 57 (top left, bottom), 58–59, 222 (top left)

Tim Hursley 23 (bottom), 100 (top left, top right, bottom left), 101, 229 (top right)

© Tom Kessler 46–47, 48, 49, 50–51, 52–53, 60 (left), 60–61 (bottom), 62–63, 65, 66–67, 80–81, 82 (bottom left), 83, 90–91, 92–93, 116–117, 118–119, 175 (bottom), 188–189, 190–191, 220 (top right, bottom right), 222 (bottom right, bottom left), 223 (top right), 224 (top right), 228 (bottom right)

Index

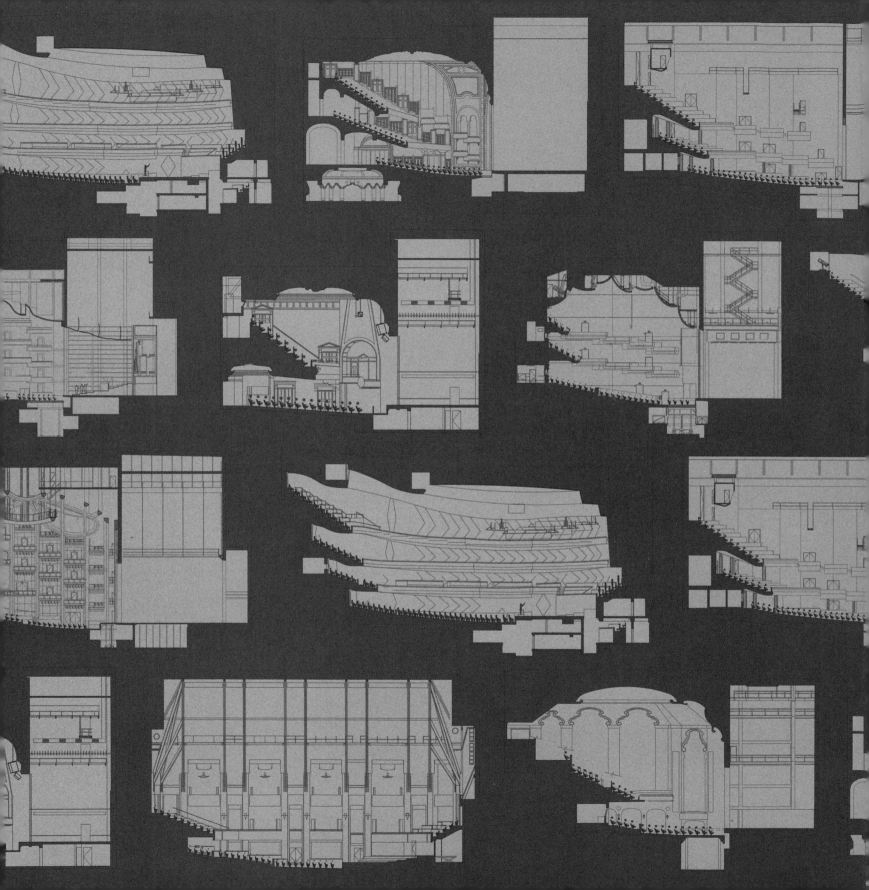